INVESTING
IN THE
U.S.

---- ★ ----

THE ULTIMATE GUIDE TO
U.S. REAL
ESTATE

REED GOOSSENS

REED GOOSSENS

WHAT OTHERS ARE SAYING

"Real estate investing is an amazing way to build wealth, yet so many people are too scared and intimidated to take the plunge. This book covers everything you need to know, from what you personally want out of real estate investing to more technical and logistical considerations, in easy-to-understand language."

Kathleen Shannon
Host of *Being Boss* podcast, entrepreneur, author, and real estate investor

• • • • • • • • •

"Want to invest in the US real estate market from abroad? Then follow the blueprint in this must-read book and learn from Reed Goossens—one of the best in the business."

Michael Blank
Multifamily investor and educator and author of *Financial Freedom with Real Estate Investing*

I dedicate this book to my late mother, my first and best mentor.

"We aren't here to f#@K spiders" – Trish Robson

This is an Australian saying and something my mother said often throughout her incredible life. It means that we aren't put on this earth to *'stuff'* around; we are here to live the fullest life possible, be bold, be brave and go out and give life a "crack." Life is short so do not waste the opportunity; live your life on your terms.

CONTENTS

FOREWORD

BY JONATHAN TWOMBLY

What my friend Reed Goossens has accomplished in just a few years is nothing short of remarkable.

He took a gamble and left a stable, well-paying career as an engineer.

He built a real estate empire that, at this writing, stands at more than $100,000,000 in assets under management—and growing.

He's become one of the leading authorities on multifamily real estate investment—and how foreign investors can break into the United States' property market—as a pioneering podcast host.

And he's done this all after moving to a foreign country and starting out with no network and little in the way of resources, other than his own talents for putting together projects and bringing together people. Having spent years abroad myself in Japan and the United Kingdom, I know from experience how hard it is to build a life from scratch in a foreign country. And, yet, while living about as far away from the place of his birth as it's possible to get and still be on Earth, Reed has thrived and built an empire.

Over the last two years, I've been fortunate to participate with Reed in a monthly telephone conference of multifamily syndication experts, and over that time I have been able to watch Reed grow as an investor and as an entrepreneur.

Not satisfied to master the real estate business as an investor, Reed has been pushing forward with innovative ideas on sourcing materials and vertically integrating his business to make his properties even more profitable for investors. Even as a very experienced real estate investor myself, it's been a deep learning experience for me to see how Reed is pushing the boundaries of creativity in his business.

You, as the reader, should be very grateful that you've obtained a copy of this book. For what you are about to read is based on the true-life experience and critical insights of an investor who has seen much, experienced much, and overcome many obstacles in building a successful real estate business. That knowledge and insight is distilled into the pages of this book.

If you are just starting out in the real estate investment business, this book will be an excellent primer for you to obtain the basic knowledge you need to start taking concrete action on your investment goals.

And if, like me, you are an experienced investor, you will find new approaches and ways of doing things that had not occurred to you, just as I have done listening to Reed on our calls, month after month over the last few years.

Read this book closely, take its lessons to heart and, most of all, put them into practice.

All the best in your real estate investing journey.

Jonathan Twombly
Two Bridges Asset Management LLC
Brooklyn, New York

CHAPTER 1
STORIES "YARNING"

"Change your story, change your life."
– Tony Robbins

As you read the quote above, you might be asking yourself if changing your life is really so simple. Or perhaps you're simply wondering why a book about real estate investing (REI) begins with a quote by author, entrepreneur, and life coach Tony Robbins.

If it's the latter, don't worry, you've still got the right book. You'll learn plenty about REI in the pages ahead. But this book is more than a simple how-to manual on REI. It's also a vehicle for you to think about your own story, which consists of the successive life events that have led you to your present condition. Each of those events has shaped who you are today, physically, emotionally, mentally, and, of course, financially.

Although I can't speak to your physical, emotional, and mental states (that's where other people, like Tony Robbins, come in), I can speak to your financial condition, which has been shaped by your past and present. And as Robbins has said, if you change your story, your financial outlook, among other aspects of your life, will change, too.

Before we go any further, however, allow me to introduce myself, which is important if I'm going to advise you on life changes and financial matters. Without a proper introduction, anything I say will ring hollow and likely be greeted with strong skepticism, if it's read at all.

To avoid such depressing scenarios, let's get down to it. Who exactly am I?

I'm Reed Goossens, civil engineer turned real estate investor. Australian born and bred, I now call the United States my home. You can take comfort in knowing that I'm more than just the author of this book.

When it comes to REI, I possess years of in-the-trenches experience. From purchasing small, inexpensive duplexes in upstate New York to syndicating multi-million-dollar apartment complexes across the US, I have amassed a diverse real estate portfolio around the country and currently serve as the principal owner of RSN Property Group and the Co-Founder of Wildhorn Capital.

In referring to my "years of experience," let me be perfectly clear about two things.

First, I'm not content to rest on the laurels of my past experiences. In other words, you're not about to read a book by an REI dinosaur whose glory days were so long ago they might as well have occurred during the Bronze Age. No, that's not me by any stretch.

Despite my involvement in more than $150 million worth of real estate deals, I am not ready for early retirement. I remain 100% in the game today. In addition to my companies, I share my knowledge of the industry through my podcast, *Investing in the US*. As of this writing, I've recorded over 130 episodes and it's clear that someone other than my 100-year-old grandmother is listening. People tune in to hear valuable advice from REI heavyweights like John Lee Dumas, David Osborn, Pat Hiban, Jake Stenziano, Joe Fairless, Kathy Fettke, Rod Khleif, and many more. Their expansive knowledge is what I would have loved to have absorbed in the early days of my own REI career, way back in 2013.

Huh?

2013?

That's right. Although I first started entertaining the idea of getting into real estate investing in 2009, I actually entered the REI game about five years ago, which leads me to the second point I want to make when I refer to my "years of experience." If you only consider those five years of experience in REI, someone like bestselling author Robert T. Kiyosaki, who wrote *Rich Dad Poor Dad* (which I first discovered in 2009 and which marked a turning point in the journey that's led me to where I am today), has me beat.

You can relax knowing I'm not the kind of person who's done a single deal, gotten lucky, and now believes he's on Kiyosaki's level. Thanks to the quality and quantity of the deals I've made, there's actual depth inside these pages and real experience that stretches well beyond just a single, lucky break.

That's not to say I didn't benefit from a lucky break. I did. But it wasn't a real estate deal. My lucky break was the realization that, with personal initiative, you can escape the rat race and achieve financial freedom. You can chart a different course for yourself. Lead a different life. Write a different story.

Story. There's that word again. Remember the quote at the beginning of this chapter?

"Change your *story*, change your life."

It speaks to what I started to realize nine years ago when I picked up *Rich Dad Poor Dad* for the first time: that it really *is* possible for anyone to take initiative, work hard, and liberate themselves from the 9-to-5 grind.

How do I know?

Because I did it within the past five years. Which, if you're paying attention, is the same time frame as my REI career.

Coincidence? Hardly. REI has been absolutely essential to my success at becoming less beholden to the restrictions of a regular day job. After taking the first steps towards breaking out on my own, REI, along with my consulting work, has afforded me the freedom to be less dependent on a traditional 9-to-5 career.

My aim with this book is to show you how REI can bring you freedom, too. To further that aim, I'll share my own story with you, which would not be complete without personal anecdotes about my life and lots of substantive REI concepts and strategies.

In the most basic sense, my story is the tale of an Australian who quit his job, moved to New York City, and built a new financially independent life from scratch.

Just a few years ago I was at the airport. My heart was racing. My hands were sweaty. And my leg was noticeably shaking.

My girlfriend noticed. Expressing concern, she asked me if I was ok and remarked that I seemed nervous.

I was too embarrassed to give a truthful answer.

Instead, I replied with a bland, "No, I'm fine," and forced a semi-smile.

Deep down, however, I *was* nervous. And for good reason. I was waiting to board a one-way international flight to the US. In just a few minutes, I'd be leaving Australia for New York City with all of my possessions and the goal of making my dream of financial independence a reality. I was determined to bite the bullet—to take action, have confidence in myself, and take a stab at putting my very limited money where my mouth was.

To be fair, this wasn't my first rodeo. Once before, I'd left Australia to pursue a new life halfway across the world in Europe. While there, I spent the majority of my early to mid-twenties chasing a multitude of opportunities. I backpacked around the continent, lived in hostels, and worked in London. I also gallivanted around the south of France, working for the world's wealthy on their obscenely expensive yachts.

This time, however, everything was different. I wasn't flying to Europe. And I wasn't about to embark on the same kinds of spontaneous adventures.

Instead, I was traveling to the US after having made a conscious decision to take control of my life. In doing so, I'd chosen to leave my job and my family behind and move, without knowing what the future would hold.

My only certainty: I knew my destination would be New York City, which I'd fallen in love with during a backpacking trip after my yachting days.

At the time, I knew that someday I'd need to live there. I wanted to experience the hustle and bustle, and live off the energy of the people. I found the young entrepreneurs particularly inspiring and in a league of their own. I wanted to live among them, as an entrepreneur myself, meeting and competing with the best in the world.

As a backpacker, the thought of pursuing my New York City dreams was exhilarating. But as I was sitting in the airport waiting to board the plane to my future, I felt a combination of excitement and fear.

My mixed emotions stemmed from knowing the vast difference between visiting a city and moving your entire life there. And moving without a job, without a detailed plan, and with limited money made my future suddenly seem terribly uncertain. Was it any wonder that I was shaking?

The truth is, I was pushing myself to make it work. To make the transition successful, I would need to be 100% committed to my goals and not look back. I had to trust myself, have faith in my decision, and believe that I could succeed no matter what.

Trusting and having confidence in yourself doesn't just apply to picking up and moving across the world. It applies to transitioning into REI, or really, into any new field. To make such a transition successful, you need to be 100% committed and never doubt yourself.

That's why this book is about more than simply REI. There's plenty of REI meat coming in later chapters. But that meat won't be very tasty unless it's seasoned with plenty of self-confidence. In other words, it's not enough to be book smart about REI. You need to possess the inner confidence to go out and "give it a crack" (Aussie for "give it a go").

This book is about having faith in yourself in any undertaking, whether it's REI or something entirely different like traveling abroad, finding a new job, or simply meeting new people. All of these things require confidence. You have to know, deep down, that things will work out because you're going to do whatever it takes to make them work out.

My story is intended as an initial shot of confidence for you. I hope I can inspire you to get off the fence and say, "If Reed can do it, so can I."

Wherever you are as you read this, know that it's possible to do this, regardless of your current circumstances, whether you're reading this book during your spare moments at a well-remunerated yet utterly dead-end job, or whether you're unemployed and are reading this while worrying about your next rent payment.

In either case, I've been in your shoes. So hear me when I tell you, once more, that it's possible to take control of your life and make the kind of massive changes you're after.

My own changes consisted of becoming an investor in US real estate. Given that I'm Australian, you might wonder why I focused on the US and why on real estate?

The answer to both questions can be found by rewinding the clock back to 2009.

At that time, I was 24 years old and nursing a major hangover that wasn't the result of a wild night of drinking with mates. Rather, I was hung over from having just spent the previous two years living abroad.

I spent the first year in London working as a structural engineer on the 2012 Olympic Games. I spent the following year backpacking around Europe and working on the yachts I mentioned earlier.

That two-year walkabout certainly had plenty of actual hangovers. Frankly, it was the wildest time of my life. If you and I ever meet, I'll have no shortage of stories to tell you over a beer. ;)

After my time in Europe, I returned to Brisbane, Australia, and traded hostels for an apartment and the yachts for a 9-to-5 job. This was when the booze-free hangover began.

As I was working as a civil engineer thousands of miles from where I'd just been, real life hit me in the face.

I can distinctly remember sitting in my cubicle at my new job on a Wednesday morning. No meetings were scheduled and although I didn't have any pressing work to do, I had a lot of busywork. But I was expected to be in my cubicle, doing the busywork until it was time to go home.

Worst of all, that day wasn't unique. I'd had other days on the job when I'd felt trapped in my cubicle. But I'd ignored my feelings and blamed them on being new to the job, sleep-deprived, and generally unmotivated.

Still, I couldn't escape the sense of being trapped. It was bloody scary really to think that society expected me to be working for someone else, in a cubicle, for the next 40 years of my life.

Sound familiar? Chances are you've had the same nauseating experience. You've probably questioned the need to work for "the man" at a 9-to-5 job for 40 or more years. I questioned it over and over again.

Don't laugh, but my first thought when I was having this crisis was, "Can't someone just pay me to live my life?"

Assessing the situation more seriously, I found myself trapped in an industry that wasn't pushing me enough. In addition, my job didn't fulfill my financial needs. Even if I had taken on another job, my net worth was still directly tied to my paycheck. And that meant more of the same drudgery.

I knew I needed to find something that would provide me enough income that I would never have to work for anyone again or, better yet, never have to work at all.

Fueled by this desire, I sought ways to generate income and make what little money I did have work for me. On numerous occasions, my search led me to websites about wealth and entrepreneurship. Of these sites, many focused on the stock market and REI. The "wealth-building" content I found elsewhere also emphasized these two areas.

Of the two sectors, I felt a greater connection to real estate. As a civil engineer, my day job already exposed me to large-scale commercial real estate developments. In addition, my dad, who is a teacher, had enjoyed a few modest successes in the Australian real estate market as an investor.

Like you, I was starting from scratch in REI. I began by Googling as much as I could about REI. Within the first month of searching, my efforts led me to Kiyosaki's landmark book *Rich Dad Poor Dad*, which opened my eyes to what "financial freedom" and "long-term wealth" really meant. Kiyosaki showed me that I could take control of my life and escape the rat race. The key was to transition from life as an employee to life as an investor.

How does Kiyosaki advise you do that? I won't spoil the book for you, but I strongly encourage you to read it if you haven't already. *Rich Dad Poor Dad* might very well be one of the most eye-opening books you've read in a long time.

I also devoted my spare time to researching REI and increasing my financial IQ. I did this by attending as many different real estate networking events as I could and surrounding myself with successful people in the industry, particularly investors.

The more I learned about REI, the more I knew it was the right industry for me and so many of the other people I met who had reached the same conclusion about their own careers. I met and read about countless successful investors who lacked my own structural engineering background and had in many cases started out with even less savings than I had (and I didn't have much).

What is it about REI that's attractive to so many people? In all of my research, the answer seems to revolve around the four main concepts (the "Big Four") that allow real estate investors to make money.

It's important to note that REI income is earned passively, meaning that it's generated without your having to expend physical effort earning it. You can devote your free time to other endeavors and the income from REI will follow. Depending on where you are in your REI career, the passive income may not be enough to support you 100%. But, if you keep at it and are successful, it can bring you complete financial freedom.

THE "BIG FOUR"

CASH FLOW

To understand "cash flow," think about a property you invest in. If the property produces rental income that exceeds the combined total of expenses and mortgage payments, you have money to spare. The leftover cash then flows to you, the investor.

This means the money you initially invested to purchase a property is now "working capital" and produces passive income. Your money works for you and you profit as a result. This turning of the tables, where your money works for you rather than you working for money, is called "cash flow." And it's only one of the major benefits of investing in real estate.

AMORTIZATION

The second element in the "Big Four" is amortization. In its simplest form, amortization occurs as your tenants, by paying rent, help pay down the principal of your mortgage on the property. As the principal owed on the mortgage decreases, your equity, or ownership, in the property increases. In a nutshell, your tenants are doing the hard work for you. Eventually, when the principal on the mortgage has been fully paid through tenants' rent payments, you'll have achieved full ownership in the property. And you'll have barely lifted a finger. Having your tenants pay down the principal certainly beats having to make those mortgage payments using your own funds, doesn't it?

APPRECIATION

The third concept on our "Big Four" list is appreciation. It's another of REI's primary benefits that you're sure to appreciate (pun intended). New investors often have a decidedly wrong view of appreciation, often thanks to the advice of "armchair investors" who possess little-to-no actual experience in the game.

For better or worse, many of us have such "trusted" sources in our own lives, the "Uncle Bobs," if you will. Folks who believe that if you buy a single-family house, the value of your house will increase over time. This concept is known as market appreciation.

The truth, however, is that there are no guarantees that such an increase will occur. The value of your real estate investment is dictated by the market cycle and the comparative values of other residential properties in the neighborhood. As an investor, you have no real control over the markets. You therefore lack control over the value of your property.

Your Uncle Bob might say, "OK, but what about good or even 'hot' markets? In those cases, it doesn't really matter that you lack control over the markets, right?"

Sorry, Bob, but the answer is still "no." That's because the model only works when everything is going well. Yet as the 2008 recession proved, the value of a single-family property can plummet in a shockingly short period of time. As an investor in 2008, you'd have potentially lost quite a bit of money. Market appreciation is great, but the potential for it shouldn't be the sole factor you rely on when investing in real estate.

This book, however, isn't interested in discussing the pros and cons of investing in single-family homes. The properties I invest in, and that I recommend my readers invest in, are commercial multifamily properties, which fall under the category of "commercial real estate." Such properties follow a standard business model.

For those unfamiliar with the model, it's expressed by a simple formula:

Value = Net Operating Income (NOI) / Capitalization (Cap) Rate

This formula focuses on two parameters: the income generated by the property (NOI) and the property's cap rate. If you control these two things, you control the value of your property. This is where "forced appreciation" comes into play.

Wondering how?

You can start by increasing rents. You won't always be able to do this, but when you identify a potential investment property, you'll want to confirm that you'll be able to bring existing rents up to market rates. That said, NOI is based on both income and on operating expenses. If you are unable to increase rents but are able to reduce operating expenses, you can still increase cash flow and "force" an increase in value of the property.

This concept is really no different from owning a more traditional business. With a traditional business, if you succeed in increasing income, the value of the business increases. This is precisely why I love investing in commercial real estate, particularly in commercial multifamily real estate.

TAX BENEFITS

Finally, no discussion of the benefits of REI would be complete without mention of the tax benefits. It's yet another reason why REI is unrivaled among other forms of investing.

The US government loves when people invest in real estate because real estate investors provide jobs and housing for the masses. As a reward for their contributions to the economy, the government offers investors substantial tax advantages and incentives.

One of the best advantages is "depreciation," which means investors can take their cash flow tax-free. In addition, the US government provides two more advantages to real estate investors. Investors can harvest the equity tax-free or postpone paying taxes on the sale of an investment to a later date.

In the second case, investors can roll over their profits into other bigger and better investments, thereby increasing their cash flow and the overall value of their portfolio. It's what we refer to as a "1031 exchange," a concept that I discuss later in this book.

The ability to roll over your profits, tax-free, into more investments to earn more money is unique. I'm no stock expert, but I do know that stock investments won't allow you to do that. On this point alone, I might rest my case for the superiority of REI as a career move. But then I'd be neglecting the other three compelling reasons—cash flow, amortization, and appreciation—discussed above. Together, these "Big Four" concepts form the basis of what makes real estate so attractive to investors for creating financial freedom and long term wealth.

If you're financially struggling to breathe, I strongly encourage you to pursue REI.

Now that you've enjoyed an interlude about the benefits of REI, let's return to my personal story. My move to New York City was an incredibly big step because I was essentially rebuilding every aspect of my adult life. Rebuilding included everything from finding housing to buying furniture to obtaining a social security number.

Between these tasks and so many others, I also had to tackle another challenge, which was arguably the biggest piece of the entire puzzle. I needed to find a job and fast. I realize this sounds ironic, since I've just spent a couple of pages criticizing 9-to-5 jobs. But I'm a pragmatist at heart and willing to do whatever it takes, within legal and ethical bounds, to succeed.

I needed a job because I'd entered the US on a temporary visa that would expire within six months unless I had work. With a job, my visa could be extended indefinitely.

Knowing this, I threw myself headfirst into the process of finding work. It was no easy feat. Unlike my American girlfriend, who has since become my wife, employers saw me as a "foreigner," which complicated my efforts. I had to hustle, and by "hustle" I mean bust my ass, to find a job. Without a job, my dream would unceremoniously end in six months when I'd be required to board a plane back to Australia.

Despite the challenge, I remained persistent, a quality I'd learned to master during my yachting days. Back then, I'd walk the docks in France before dawn every morning in order to find day work. Time and again, I'd get the same answer: "Non, merci."

No. No. No. And then, suddenly, a "Oui!"

Having met frequent rejection like this early on in my adult life, I was completely comfortable with it. I learned that the "yes" would eventually come. It always does, with enough persistence. And when you get that "yes," it can change your story and open the door to the next chapter in your life

In New York, I applied the same persistence to my job search. I also took a different tactical approach to landing a paycheck. I avoided applying online to engineering firms, which is the equivalent to throwing your resume into a black hole. Instead, I Googled "engineering firms NYC" and strategically targeted small to midsize outfits that weren't large enough to have HR departments or other gatekeepers.

After creating a list of 40 firms, I printed a pile of resumes and hit the streets. I literally walked into offices even if they weren't hiring. I did this repeatedly and encountered a good deal of rejection. I spent entire days in this manner, hitting the streets to find a job. Eventually, after three weeks of this, I received one "maybe."

That particular firm didn't actually have a vacant position, but they were looking to expand. Plus, they liked the fact that I just showed up and requested to meet with management.

That was how, within six weeks of arriving in New York City, I had a job. With gainful employment, I had completed Step 1 of my transition to a new life.

Step 2 was to start educating myself about US REI.

After settling into the new job, I quickly sought out REI clubs and networking events. My goal was to surround myself with like-minded REI people.

I can still remember attending my first REI networking event in New York City. It was an intoxicating experience, and not just because drinks were served. I arrived thinking REI events in the US would be like those in Australia. Imagine my surprise to find that networking events in the Big Apple were like Australia's best events, but on steroids. I'd never experienced anything like it before. Fast-talking Americans discussing all things REI. The thought of it gets my blood racing even now.

I loved every minute of that first event and all the other events I attended. Nonetheless, I quickly realized that I needed to do more than just attend. It was essential for me to learn investing lingo, and fast. Otherwise I wouldn't be able to swim with these seasoned real estate sharks.

To educate myself, I began learning everything I could about investing in the US market. Sadly, a certain podcast called "Investing in the US" (my own) had yet to exist. Instead, I turned to books, by the truckload.

Among the many books I read: *Rich Dad Poor Dad*, *How to Win Friends and Influence People* by Dale Carnegie, *The Fundamentals of Investing* by Scott B. Smart, Lawrence J. Gitman, Michael D. Joehnk, and *The 4-Hour Workweek* by Timothy Ferriss. These books and the others I read taught me basic REI vocabulary and covered various advanced topics important for understanding the industry.

Go to www.reedgoossens.com/investing-in-the-us-the-ultimate-guide-to-us-real-estate for links.

I spent a solid year immersing myself in books, attending events, and getting to know the lay of the REI landscape. The more I studied, the more I realized just how different REI is in the US compared to Australia. Three differences stood out.

First, barriers to entry in the US are considerably lower than in many other developed countries. Compared to Australia, for example, the US erects fewer obstacles to finding and investing in properties with great cash flow.

Second is the difference in yield. For REI, the US offers a better yield. Since property prices outside the major cities are lower, cash flow is more prevalent.

Finally, Americans like to refer to their currency as the "almighty dollar" and there's some truth in that. The US dollar is the world's currency. Investors around the world like America's stable government and the opportunity to invest in US dollars.

The differences between US REI and REI in countries like Australia became clear to me as I educated myself. Eventually, I was ready to shift from learning mode to action mode. I continued to educate myself, of course, but I was ready to break out of the "analysis paralysis" stage and find and make my first deal.

That was just five years ago. But in those five years... let's just say there's enough material for a book.

I've written this book because I want you to be in a better position to change your life and engage in REI than I was when I first started out. I want you to be better prepared not only mentally and have more confidence in yourself than I did, but also be better prepared conceptually.

I hope this introductory chapter has lit a spark in you. My goal for the rest of this book is to nurture that spark into a roaring bonfire so you're able to begin your REI career in a blaze of glory.

We haven't met, and you don't know me. But I promise you these aren't just empty, feel-good words. I truly mean every one of them. I intend to share as much valuable material as is required to help make you successful.

I'd love to take this journey with you if you're game. If you care to join me, read on to the next chapter where you'll learn how to find "hot" real estate markets.

COMFORT CHALLENGE

At the end of each chapter, I'm going to be giving you a "comfort challenge." Think of these challenges as a kind of homework assignment. The goal is to get you to take action on what you're learning in the book, so you can begin to walk the walk while you learn to talk the talk.

Ready for the first comfort challenge? As it's the first chapter, your first comfort challenge is simple:

Pack up everything you own, quit your job, and move halfway around the world. Easy, right?

Just kidding.

The true comfort challenge for this chapter is much easier. For the first challenge, attend two real estate networking events this month and during each of the next two months. At these six events, try and meet as many people as you can. Your goal is to surround yourself with active real estate investors and immerse yourself in the REI world, just as I did upon arriving in NYC. You can Google local groups in your area. If you live in LA or New York, check out the "Downtown Los Angeles Real Estate Network" (my own group) or "NYREIA" (a group led by Nick Tang).

★ ★ AUSSIE-ISMS ★ ★

Given the differences between Australian English and American English, I'd like to share some great "Aussie-isms" with you. At the end of each chapter, you'll find a few phrases or terms that are quintessentially Australian.

For chapter one, here are a few:

1. "Yarning" – Aussie slang for telling stories; conversations.

2. "She'll be right" – Everything will work out in the end. You must believe this if you decide to leap into REI.

3. "Chockers" – Crammed, packed. How those NYC networking events felt, with so many attendees!

4. "Blokes" – Guys. Men are not the only ones who can succeed at REI; it's a co-ed pursuit!

5. "Give it a crack" – Give it a go; make it happen.

CHAPTER 2

WHY INVEST IN US REAL ESTATE?

OK, story time's over. Let's get down to business. In the chapter ahead, we're going to look at some broad concepts in and around REI. My goal is to give you a "30,000-foot view" of REI, so you can see this investment area as it is. From the conceptual, we'll then begin our descent into specific REI topics in later chapters.

To kick things off here, let's start by answering a basic question:

IS REAL ESTATE FOR YOU?

You'll have to decide for yourself. What I can tell you is that investing in real estate has enabled many of today's wealthy to achieve their success, including myself. Look around in your community and, chances are, you can spot someone whose wealth can be linked to REI.

And that's just at the local grassroots level. If we look at REI on a larger scale, there's no shortage of success stories. Today's headliners include everyone from Warren Buffet to Robert Kiyosaki to Arnold Schwarzenegger. Buffet and Kiyosaki are probably two people you'd expect to have become wealthy through REI. But Schwarzenegger? While we think of him as an actor and bodybuilder, his first million didn't come from either. Instead, he made it by investing in multi-family apartment buildings in Los Angeles.

Those three, by the way—Buffet, Kiyosaki, and Schwarzenegger—are also just today's headliners. If you look even further back, you'll find no shortage of REI success stories. People like John D. Rockefeller, William Zeckendorf, and Henry Flagler.

Zecken-who? William Zeckendorf, as in the developer behind Century City in Los Angeles and the Magnificent Mile in Chicago. And Flagler? Only the real estate investor who helped create Miami, Florida.

Your own REI efforts don't have to match those of today's and yesterday's headliners. My point in sharing their names is merely to convey the scale upon which this game can be played.

Let's tone things down, though, at least in the beginning. The wealth can come, no doubt. But you need to recognize that REI is about more than just making money. I say that for two reasons.

First, as you'd expect, obsessing only on money tends to be a bad idea. Beyond that, REI is about building lasting wealth, over the long term, which works for you beyond any quick payday. The kind of lasting wealth, I'd add, that enables you to never have to exchange your time for a paycheck again. The most valuable asset in your life is time; time is the only thing money can't buy.

To build wealth like that, you'll need to think long term. As you do, there are some other considerations to weigh. Considerations that will help you to further answer our earlier question: "Is real estate for you?"

But before you answer that question, let's dive into the nuts and bolts of why I love REI to help build financial freedom and long-term wealth.

If you didn't know, there are seven fundamental ways in which you can get your money working for you using REI. These four fundamentals aren't found in any other investment opportunity. Certain elements can be found in other investments, like stocks and bonds. However, the power of all four combined is only found in real estate.

THE SEVEN FUNDAMENTALS OF REAL ESTATE INVESTING:

We all want our money working as hard as we do in our day jobs, but what work is our money doing if we invest in real estate? And how does investing in real estate mean we can establish a secondary income that can one day lead to financial freedom? Let's define the four fundamentals of REI. I want you to use these fundamentals when comparing any investment opportunity.

1. Appreciation

There are two types of appreciation to consider when it comes to REI. The first is driven by the market, also known as *market appreciation*. Some people also refer to market appreciation as *neutral appreciation*. It's an increase in the value of real estate over time. This increase can occur as a result of various factors, including increased demand or weakening supply, or as a result of changes in inflation or interest rates. This type of appreciation is out of our control as an investor. Market appreciation is nice but should never be the sole reason you invest in real estate; "hoping" that your investment will one day be worth more than what you originally paid for it can be a losing formula. Take the crash in 2008 for example. The average person who purchased a property in 2006 and 2007 saw their properties valued considerably less than what they paid for them by 2008. This is a prime example of market-dictated appreciation (in this case, depreciation), and in the case of 2008, it meant a major loss for a lot of home owners and investors across the US. Investors had no control over the value of their assets as the market took a nose dive.

Coming from Australia, I was always told that properties would *double their value every ten years.* Has anyone else heard this? I will not argue with it. If you look at history, properties do appreciate over time due to changes in the local market, which can lead to increased value, but this is outside of our control as an investor. Thus, my advice is to think of **market appreciation** as a "bonus." If it happens, great, but you should never solely count on this type of appreciation when investing in real estate.

The second type of appreciation is what you as an investor create. It's called *forced appreciation*, and it's why I like commercial multifamily real estate assets more than single-family housing.

Forced appreciation is the change of income produced by a property (the asset) as a result of changing the way you operate your property. When assessing a new investment opportunity, you must always look for ways to "tweak the machine," or to make changes that will increase your income, decrease your operating expenses, and thus increase the overall value of the property. These "tweaks" are controlled by the investors, not by the market. The underlying value in commercial real estate is that these assets are viewed as "businesses," and the formula for valuing a business is as follows:

Operating Expense Ratio = Operating Expenses (OPEX) / Net Sales

Without getting lost in the weeds of accounting jargon, the above formula simply means: if you control the operating expenses and increase the sales, you directly increase the value of your "business," in this case, a commercial real estate asset.

Another way of looking at the above formula is:

Value = NOI / Cap Rate

NOI = Gross income − operating expenses

Cap Rate = Capitalization rate: this is the return on your money if you were to pay all-cash for a property. Your local market will have a "market cap rate," and this should be used when defining the value of a property.

Example:

Let's say you are looking at a five-unit building to purchase, and you notice the "in-place" rents for each apartment are $25/month below what other units are renting for in the local neighborhood. If you charge tenants $25/month more in rent, you have increased the income of the property (i.e.: the net sales). Let's assume the following:

- Monthly expenses: $100/month/unit (total = $500/month, $6,000/year)
- Current Rent: $250/unit/month (total = $1,250/month, $15,000)
- Market Cap Rate = 7%

In-place value of the asset = NOI ($15,000 - $6,000) / 7% = $128,571

If we increase the rent by $25/month/unit, and leave the current OPEX as is, the new value of the property is:

Value = New NOI ($16,500 - $6,000) / 7% = $150,000

So, by simply increasing the rents to match the local market ($25/

unit/month) I was able to "force" the value of the property up by approximately $21,430 of value. Pretty impressive, right? In this example, I only focused on the income proportion of the equation, but you also look at ways to reduce the OPEX of a property. Reducing OPEX has the same effect on the value of the property. Think of it this way: For every dollar you increase the NOI, you directly increase the value of the property by $1 if the property is in a market with a cap rate of 10%.

Now apply the same thought process to a 50-unit or even a 100-unit apartment building. Scalability is key!

2. Cash Flow

This is the holy grail for any investor, and it is the definition of "getting your money to work for you."

Cash flow is the money left over that you can put in your pocket after paying for all operating expenses and debt services on the property.

Why is cash flow so important?

Cash flow from an investment property is paramount to establishing a secondary income, which will hopefully lead to financial freedom one day. The goal of investing in cash-flowing assets is to create enough secondary income to match your current primary income from your day job. This is known as creating financial freedom. If your assets produce the same, or more, income than your day job then why do you need a day job? I use cash flow to help me free up my most valuable asset: my time.

Think of investing for cash flow as the foundation for any strong real estate investment portfolio. Take the "food triangle" for establishing a good diet that leads to a healthy life. You remember the one they showed you as a kid in school?

We all know that the bottom-most layer of the food triangle is full of foods that are good for us; fruits, vegetables, grains, etc. This layer forms the basis of a good healthy diet. The further up the food triangle, the less healthy the foods are, (ex: meats, dairy, sweets, sugars, etc.). Of course you can eat these foods at the top of the food triangle, but they should be consumed in moderation with a focus on eating more foods from the bottom layer.

The same is true when it comes to your real estate portfolio. The bottom-most layer should be filled with cash-flowing properties that will form the basis of a "healthy" portfolio. As we ascend up the "portfolio triangle," risk increases. You should always focus on putting cash-flowing properties in the bottom layer of your portfolio. The more cash-flowing properties in the bottom layer, the closer you get to financial freedom, which means that you can go off and do riskier deals like flipping houses and getting involved in ground-up construction. Both types of investing can be very lucrative, but they both carry higher levels of risk as compared to a cash-flowing asset.

How to analyze if a property's cash flows?

A cash-flow analysis is simple: The gross income must be more than the outgoing expenses.

Example:

> Gross income = $2,000 /month
> OPEX = $1,200
> Debt Services (mortgage) = $500/month
>
> Cash flow = $2,000 - $1,200 - $500 = $300/month. In later chapters, I will discuss how to know if your OPEX is too high, and what you can do about it.

Remember to always focus on cash flow.

3. Amortization:

The third fundamental of REI, which tends to get overlooked when analyzing a potential investment, is the equity accumulation as a result of the tenants paying your mortgage for you. In the cash flow section, we defined the benefits of putting money in your pocket but coupled with paying off your debt services (monthly mortgage payments), your tenants are effectively reducing the principal balance of the loan on the property, thus increasing the equity in the property. Show me a stock investment where you can borrow money from the bank, use it to buy stocks, and then have the stocks pay your principal and have cash flow at the same time?

4. Depreciation:

The fourth REI fundamental also tends to be overlooked during high-level analysis of a potential investment. Depreciation is the reduction of an asset's value over a period. In simple terms, the value of a house built today will not be the same in five years' time. Things lose their value over time. So does real estate.

In the taxation world, the US government has defined a useful life for different real estate assets: for residential real estate, the useful life is 27.5 years and for commercial real estate, the useful life is 35 years. Yes, this may seem arbitrary, but let's look at an example.

Let's say you buy a single-family home for $200,000. The tax assessor's estimate of the land value is $65,000, and the building value estimate is $135,000. The depreciation expense that you take each year against rental income would be $135,000 divided by the IRS-allowed 27.5 years of useful life. This gives you a depreciation expense each year of $4,909 ($135,000 / 27.5 years). So thanks to that depreciation expense, you are saving $4,909 multiplied by your marginal tax rate (a topic for another day). This could be tax savings from $1,000 to $2,000 per year, just for the depreciation amount.

The calculation and write-off are pretty straightforward, but the actual tax savings amount gets a little more complicated depending on your situation and income. Many people fudge this calculation from the start, so it's best to find a licensed tax professional and start saving some money going forward. Know that depreciation through owning real estate can put additional money in your pocket and offset your taxable income.

5. Hedge Against Inflation

Another reason why people invest in real estate, particularly commercial real estate, is that it can be an excellent hedge against inflation. In other words, you benefit from inflation. Why? Say you invest $100k today into a commercial asset. That same $100k in five years' time will be hedged against inflation because your investment is backed by a hard asset. With the correct investment strategy, like forced appreciation, you can increase that $100k investment over time. Compare this to leaving your money in a bank, for example. $100k today will be worth less in five years' time.

6. Leverage

This REI fundamental is the biggest benefit of using real estate as a vehicle to financial freedom: "Other People's Money" (OPM) or leverage. There are a few forms of leverage that investors can take advantage of.

The first is simple: The bank! Most investors will want to maximize their leverage opportunity by using a loan to purchase their assets. Paying all-cash for an asset is fine, and there are some people out there who do that, but you need a boat load of money if you are going to buy multiple investment properties to build out your portfolio. This isn't practical for most people and will result in the journey to financial freedom taking even longer.

In the US, banks use a system known as a credit score to rank your ability as a borrower to pay back debt. When I first moved to the US, I had no idea about credit scores, and mine was nonexistent because I came from Australia. Thus, for the first few properties I purchased, I wasn't able to leverage the bank's money. Instead, I had to pay all-cash. The better your credit, the better chance you have of securing a good fixed-rate loan with low-interest rates.

Establishing credit in the US can take time, and in my case, I went the non-conventional route of establishing solid relationships with local community banks in the cities where I purchased my first two properties. Over a period of six months, I deposited my rental checks in bank accounts I had set up at these local community banks, meanwhile establishing my credit score. After six months of depositing checks, I approached the local bank manager and asked if I could refinance some of my capital out of my deals to continue growing my portfolio. The reason I chose to work with a smaller bank, rather than a larger national bank, was that the bank managers and loan officers—the people who were ultimately going to grant me a refi loan— were all based in the area I was purchasing. They were true "locals" and knew the streets and neighborhoods where I was buying and the demographics of the people to whom I was renting. Combining a "relationship first" type of approach with my bank managers, along with proof that my small initial portfolio was producing healthy cash flow, helped me break into the world of "leverage" and start using OPM to grow.

When using debt and loans to acquire assets, you typically aim to use loans to pay between 60–70% of the purchase price. Being "overleveraged" can add undue risk to your deal. Having your own equity in the deal is important, as it shows the banks you have "skin in the game." There is less chance you will walk away from an asset if you have paid for 25–30% of the cost with your own money.

The other type of leverage is created by pooling investors' money together to take down larger assets, like a 100-unit apartment building. This is also known as syndication investing. With syndication, multiple investors get to own a segment of a larger deal, with greater cash flow. I will talk more about this type of leverage in Chapter 9.

7. Deferred Taxes

Here in the US, your money's tax-free status is explained by the 1031 Exchange. This is named after Section 1031 of the Internal Revenue Code. You don't have to read the code and all of its boring government jargon. Just understand that it discusses how real estate investors can hold off on paying capital gains taxes when selling one of their investment properties. For this to happen, three conditions have to be met. The conditions that cause the 1031 Exchange to go into effect are:

1. The real estate property is an investment and not the primary residence of the investor.

2. The real estate property can be swapped for a property of the same or similar kind.

3. For replacements (i.e., swapping), there must be certain time frames in place that the investor must adhere to.

To make sure you understand the 1031 Exchange, let me explain it again in different terms. When an investor takes profits from one property sale and invests them in another property, they can defer paying taxes on the capital gains, rolling their profits into more real estate and growing their portfolio. The investor can then work on getting additional equity and more income and profits from additional property rentals. This is also a great way of scaling your real estate portfolio into large properties, tax-free, which will lead to long-term wealth.

Get the picture? As you can see, there are many benefits to investing in real estate that can help you escape the rat race, attain financial freedom, and establish long-term wealth. Show me another investment that can combine all those benefits!

CHANGING NEGATIVE CASH FLOW TO POSITIVE CASH FLOW AND CREATING MASSIVE AMOUNTS OF VALUE!

Now let's cover some ways to turn your cash flow from negative to positive.

One way is to implement a rent increase. If you take this approach, make sure you understand the local market. Know what the local market rent is and where the rents at your property stand in relation to local comps. If there's a gap between these figures, you may have an opportunity to raise rents. Still, don't get carried away. Despite how tempting it seems in the short term to raise rents significantly, only increase the rent to the amount of the current market. Any more and you may lose your tenants, and your vacancy may increase.

Raising rent isn't the only way to turn your cash flow positive. Another option is to make your tenants pay for the utilities that they use. This can relieve a major financial burden on you as the property owner. It's also easy to justify to the tenants themselves. After all, since they're living in your property, they will be using utilities every day, so it's only natural that they should be paying for these utilities. There are third-party businesses that helps multifamily property owners bill back utilities. The process is known as RUBS: Ratio Utility Billing System. Refer to the *Resources* page at the end of the book for more info. Note: implementing a RUB system may also deter tenants. Be sure to see if other properties in your local market have implemented RUBS. You will have an easier time justifying this to tenants if they have.

Along with utilities and rent increases, property taxes are another great tool for cash flow correction. Go over to your property tax assessor and see if you can find anything you've missed before. You may find that you're overpaying on taxes. If so, paying the lower, correct amount can improve your cash flow.

A final strategy I'd recommend is to contact your insurance company. See about raising your deductible. Then inquire about getting a better deal for coverage on the property. Insurance carriers, over time, tend to implement "insurance creep," which means that your premium slowly gets more and more expensive over time for the same product. If you haven't filed a claim, which would naturally bring your insurance rates up, make sure you shop around to get the most competitive price.

The four strategies I've just highlighted can each pull your cash flow out of the red and into the black. The strategies here are not, however, the only things you can do. Depending on your situation, there are likely other tactics you can employ. Such tactics would be unique to your particular situation, and I can't do justice to all of them here. The best I can do is leave you with an analogy for thinking about cash-flow correction.

In our analogy, your multifamily property is a rusty machine. The machine still works, but its glory days are long gone. Or are they? That's where you come in. Approaching this rusty machine, you tweak the knobs, give it some TLC, and restore it to its former glory. You bring the machine back to those glory days, and perhaps take it beyond too, with greater efficiency. The result then is a machine that works as good or better than it ever has.

Like the machine in this analogy, your property could be just as "rusty." Often, you'll find "rust" at older multifamily properties, where the owners haven't made the highest and best use of the property. Instead of running it like a well-oiled machine, the management is using inefficient, outdated, or even sloppy practices. Accordingly, the management is missing income, and they can conceivably gain it back just by reducing overhead and creating new cash flows.

All of this creates a golden opportunity for you, the investor. Many, many golden opportunities, in fact. Each of which is likely to be unique to your particular situation. Which is why it is important for you to fully comprehend REI's advantages and how you can benefit from all of them. To do that, let's look now at why people invest in real estate.

USING REAL ESTATE INVESTMENTS AS PASSIVE INCOME

Focus on the long term, and you'll build wealth and passive income. REI is not a get-rich-quick scheme. It's getting rich slowly. You'll also have the unique advantage of being able to profit from down markets. Investors profit during the supposed "down" times by scooping up assets that have been listed at "fire sale" prices. I can't speak to everything you'd do in a down market, but let's say that a long-term thinker finds the silver lining in such clouds. And for such investors, there's nothing "bad" about a "bad economy" or an economic downturn.

You don't have to be an opportunist, though. Hang in there, stay on top of your business, and the passive income and wealth will come.

Eventually, you'll make enough money from the rentals on your properties that you won't have to work a full-time job anymore.

Moving ahead, let's see some of the ways that you can profit from your long-term real estate investments.

PROFITING WITH REAL ESTATE INVESTMENTS

As you might expect, cash flow is at the top of our "ways to profit from REI" list. It feels bloody good to have a stream of money from a rental property entering your bank account each month.

Cash flow from a single property is excellent, but why stop there? Why not acquire more rental properties? The more you "push the envelope," the more you'll have actual envelopes (containing rent checks!) being pushed to you. These cash flows are usually protected against market downturns. There are still risks in buying and maintaining the properties. But it's no riskier than what you'd typically expect as an investor.

As you accumulate properties, you may want to pause occasionally and take stock of what you have. Look at your present portfolio and identify rental properties you own that might be spruced up. Renovating or redecorating a place increases its value and can lead to far more interest from prospective renters.

Look, as well, for other opportunities to maintain and refine your rental properties. In all likelihood, some time and attention on your part will reveal new ways to make them even more profitable.

When you're ready to get back in "buying mode," here are some general concepts you'll find useful. These concepts cover key areas that you'll likely be wondering about as you build your rental property portfolio.

BUYING UNDERVALUED REAL ESTATE

"You make money when you buy, not when you sell!"

Many a real estate investor has profited from this simple advice. Keep it at the forefront of your mind whenever you think of buying. You can profit tremendously by purchasing property that's considered to be undervalued. Not only does it save you money (compared to the higher-priced property), it can also pay off for you in the end.

But wait, you say, isn't a property that seems undervalued potentially too good to be true? It can't be that easy, can it?

In response, the short answer is YES. Sure, there are scams in REI. Loads of them. It's also true that properties at a seemingly incredible price can have major flaws that explain why they're a supposed "steal."

The truly skilled investor recognizes that scams and too-good-to-be-true properties do exist. Such an investor also understands that many properties do sell below—often well below —their actual value.

Here are some commons reasons for that:

- Foreclosed property
- The owner wants to get rid of it
- The property was passed down from a previous generation(s)
- The property is in bad shape and needs loads of repairs
- Personal events in the owner's family make them unable to care for the property
- Excessive damage has occurred from inclement weather or fire

The reasons above are the ones you hear about most. Given the range of reasons, there's probably at least a few that explain undervalued properties around you.

Undervalued properties can be great, but make sure buying them will work for you. Not every investor finds that undervalued properties serve their best interests. Sometimes a property that's average or even higher-priced may be more in line with your goals. This is especially true if you don't have the resources on hand to increase the value of an undervalued property. After all, if you can't increase the value, you'll find it difficult to come out with a profit.

Wondering where you can find undervalued properties? These properties are out there, but if you can't find any—or you want to broaden your choices—look in urban areas.

WHY US REAL ESTATE? THE GLOBAL PERSPECTIVE

I have spoken about the benefits of investing in real estate, but let's focus specifically on why people like to invest in the US.

Being an "outsider" (in Aussie slang, you're called a *Jaffa*, which is a derogatory term for an Aussie) investing in the US enables me to see the incredible benefits the US real estate market has to offer in comparison to other first-world developed countries, like Australia. I have lived in England, France, and the US and have seen the pros and cons of investing in each country. The US has a combination of factors that you can't find in other first-world countries (a magic combination of both cash flow and appreciation). If you are an American reading this and sitting on the fence—don't! Get off the fence and start educating yourself on where and how to get involved because you live in a country that is the "land of opportunity for REI."

Let's review the exact reasons why the US is a perfect environment for investing:

1. **The US provides stable and regulated markets** – Even with

the wave of anti-globalization sentiment around the world, like Brexit in the UK, for many international investors, the US is seen as a safe haven due to a diverse economy and investment opportunities coupled with a healthy balance of imports and exports, creating a relatively stable economy. All of these factors, combined with highly regulated markets, a stable US dollar, and slowing economies around the world, makes the US a relatively low-risk investment for investors compared to other global options.

2. **Global investment supports strong economies** – The US prides itself on being the *"land of opportunity,"* and given how easy it is to invest globally, the US encourages global investment within its borders. This allows international investors the opportunity to diversify their portfolio with US-based investments as well as shelter income from some countries that want to restrict capital flight.

3. **Physical, performing assets and favorable lending** – When I first moved to the US, I had no idea what a "multifamily" asset was. Some smaller multifamily assets do exist in Australia (with two to six units), but the inventory of large, commercial, multifamily assets (+100 units) in the US was something I wasn't used too. These large assets don't exist in Australia.

Also, banks and lending institutions view commercial multifamily assets like businesses, based off the net operating income (NOI). This means that if investors can control the NOI, they can control the cash flow and the value of the asset—a very powerful investment combination.

Furthermore, the US has a more favorable lending environment and more options when it comes to obtaining leverage. Specifically, non-recourse debt options are available in the US for commercial assets. Non-recourse debt is a type of loan secured by collateral, which refers to specific kinds of physical assets. If the borrower defaults, the issuer can seize the collateral but isn't allowed to seek any further compensation from the borrower, even if the collateral does not cover the full value of the defaulted amount.

4. **Capital movement restrictions and fluctuating currencies:** Some developing countries (like China, India, and South Africa, to name a few) have applied restrictions on how much capital their citizens can move from their home country to invest in the US. The reason these governments apply these restrictions is to avoid fluctuating currencies and overheated inflation. Given these restrictions, and the fact that the US dollar is a stable currency, investors from these countries desperately want to place their capital in the US to preserve their capital and wealth.

So the US has a wide-open door for REI opportunity because of this special combination of factors. Now that you know that, it's almost foolish not to take advantage of it. But it's not simple, and it's not for people who need instant gratification. You need to do your homework, and part of the homework is learning a special set of vocabulary words.

NOT EVERYBODY PLAYS THE FOOL

To avoid looking foolish, it helps to know what you're talking about when it comes to REI. That way you don't end up spouting gibberish you think is correct. Nor are you dazed and confused when a fellow investor describes one of their recent deals. Both have happened to me. I have the analogous "bruises" to prove it. In neither case did the laughter from others and my mental anguish kill me. Rather it drove me to further strengthen my understanding of real estate investment lingo.

You, as a reader, can now benefit from my study of the lingo. In the next chapter, I'll share the specific lingo that's most important for you as a real estate investor. Read on, and you'll be speaking confidently in no time.

COMFORT CHALLENGE

Let's get you taking more action. Push that comfort zone of yours ever further. Transform you into a confident real estate investor. You still don't have to, as I jokingly suggested, quit your job and move halfway around the world. What I'd prefer you do is go online and visit Rentometer.com. It's a website where you can see rent prices for various US locales.

Enter an address, and Rentometer will tell you what the properties around the address are renting at. For you, the aspiring investor, Rentometer's info will allow you to begin thinking more clearly about where to invest. You won't have to wonder what people are paying for rent in various areas. Rents will be clear to you, and you can then begin planning accordingly.

FREE "TOP BLOKE" GIFTS, CONTENT, AND DOWNLOADS

As I am a top bloke (aka a good guy), throughout this book you will find a bunch of free content that you can listen to, or download, to help you keep on track towards your investing goals.

For my first **"Top Bloke"** gift, check out and complete the following:

1. Listen to one of my earlier podcast episodes where I speak with a good mate of mine Frank Roessler, from Ashcroft Capital, about why we both love investing in large multifamily properties and the power of changing NOI to create long-term wealth. Here is the link: www.reedgoossens.com/rg-003-why-i-love-multi-family-investing-here-in-the-u-s-with-frank-roessler/

2. Download your FREE Portfolio Triangle poster to stick on your vision board, designed to be a visual reminder to help you keep on track towards your health portfolio diet.

★★ AUSSIE-ISMS ★★

What would this chapter be without some Aussie-isms? For this batch, here are three:

1. "Top Bloke" – A guy or gal who is down-to-earth, humble, and always willing to help others where they can.

2. "Ute" – A utility truck or pickup truck; What the tradie, a tradesperson, drives.

3. "You Little Ripper" – Really great.

CHAPTER 3

UNDERSTANDING US INVESTING LINGO

It is said that among the Inuit people, laughter is considered the best punishment for stealing. Not imprisonment, not physical punishment, but laughter from everyone who sees the thief, whenever that person goes out in public. Why? It's probably because the Inuit understand how much it hurts to be laughed at.

Of course they're not alone in this understanding. It never feels good to be laughed at, and no one wants to experience that.

Where's all this heading? My goal is to keep you, the aspiring real estate investor, from being laughed at. You may not initially know as much as those who have been doing this longer, but with the information you're learning now, you'll have a good foundation for growing your knowledge and skills. The only laughter you should hear is your own, as you "laugh all the way to the bank."

Let's get you started with a discussion about the essential lingo of US real estate investing.

First things first: don't assume that American real estate is the same as real estate in your own country. I made this mistake when I first touched down in the US. While in Australia, I'd spent a number of years learning about Aussie REI. Studying the Australian scene, I'd come to view REI as an appreciation play only. This outlook made sense because there were far more opportunities for appreciation than cash flow in Australia.

In the US, however, it's a different story. The American scene gives investors plenty of chances for appreciation plays, like its Australian counterpart, but investors aren't limited to focusing primarily on appreciation. Investing for cash flow is also a very viable, desired option for most investors who seek to invest in US real estate.

As an investor, it's important to understand cash flow and how it correlates to US real estate, as well as to your personal investing goals. Otherwise, you might be lost, as I was, when you hear American investors talk about cash flow. Their words may very well sound like a foreign language to you.

To better understand US REI and its lingo, let's start with the term "cash flow" itself. To remember this term, think about the classic all-American saying, "Cash is king." The saying applies to REI because "Cash *flow* is king." This isn't hyperbole—cash flow really is king! It's what will allow you to create financial freedom and help you leave your day job, so you can have more access to your most valuable asset… *your time*. Keep your eyes on your cash flow regardless of whether you're hunting for a shopping mall in the suburbs, a large multifamily home, or a duplex. Cash flow and its basic principles will be the same.

Let's move on to some of the other American investing jargon you'll need to understand to work successfully in the US. I hope you brought an appetite for learning. The content ahead will give you a lot to digest.

CAP RATE (AKA CAPITALIZATION RATE)

If you're going to succeed as a real estate investor, you need to know the value of properties (i.e., assets). Understand a property's value, and you'll have a clear sense of what you can pay for it. You can then compare its value with those of other properties. Doing so will enable you to see whether a given property is overvalued or undervalued, when measured against comparable properties in the area.

An overvalued property, as you might expect, is probably not a wise investment. The property's overly high value means you, as an investor, won't be making money. Remember, you make money when you buy, not when you sell. An undervalued property, on the other hand, is a potential opportunity.

How do you know a property's value? It comes down to two things: capitalization rate (aka cap rate) and net operating income (NOI).

The capitalization, or "cap" rate, is a term that is used frequently when discussing real estate asset sales and purchases. The cap rate is a ratio of two variables—net operating income and the current value or sale price of a property—and it helps to determine the potential return on an investment. Put another way, the cap rate is the rate at which the net operating income recapitalizes the assets value on an annual basis. In laymen terms It's the return on investment if you paid all-cash for a property. The cap rate is often used to assess real estate investment opportunities and draw conclusions across different asset classes. For instance, if you compare a multifamily deal to a self-storage deal, both can produce cash flow, and both have a corresponding cap rate.

Yeah, this is some great corner -- you wouldn't believe the cap rate.

CartoonStock.com

As an illustration, let's say you have a cap rate of 7%. You would then make 7% ROI (return on investment) if you paid all-cash.

Cap rates vary between different US markets, depending on the level of perceived risk in that market. New York City, for example, has cap rates between 1% and 3%, depending where in the city you are looking. It's a low cap rate because plenty of people want to live there, hence the perceived risk is lower. It's simple supply vs demand; there isn't enough supply to meet demand. Detroit, on the other hand, is a city that far fewer people are excitedly planning a move to. Accordingly, Detroit's cap rate is about 8–15%.

Cap rate can also be plugged into the following formula: Cap Rate = Net Operating Income (NOI) / Current Market Value (or sales price)

We can then rearrange the formula so it's focused on "current market value." This value will be what a particular property is worth.

Value = NOI / Cap Rate

Looking at this formula, you can see that the clear driver of a property's value is the NOI. That's because as NOI increases in the formula, the value of the property also increases.

Example: If an apartment building in Los Angeles has an NOI of $500,000 and the owner wants to sell the building for $12,000,000 then the cap rate is:

$500,000 / $12,000,000 = 4.17%

This "building cap rate" can be compared to the "market cap rate" of the submarket.

For example: If we know other comparable apartment buildings trade for 5% cap rate, then we know the seller of the apartment building in the previous example is asking too much for the property.

You can determine the maximum market value of the apartment building by using the "market cap rate" with the in-place NOI of the building:

NOI (in-place) / Market Cap Rate = Fair Market Value

$500,000 / 5% = $10,000,000

Now you can see that the seller may be asking too much for their property, and hence if you purchase the property at the seller's "asking price" of $12 million, you may be overpaying.

HOW ELSE ARE CAP RATES USED TO VALUE INVESTMENTS?

In the previous example, I illustrated the difference between what a seller wants to sell their property for and what the market value of the property is, which helps you as an investor determine if you will overpay.

Another way cap rates are used is to compare assets in different markets. Example: I could buy an apartment building in Los Angeles at a 5% cap rate, or I could buy the same size apartment building in Dallas-Fort Worth for $7,142,000 at a 7% cap rate and spend the remaining money buying a retail strip mall in Kansas City at a 6.5% cap rate. Looking purely at the numbers, I can decide if I want to buy one asset in a "top tier" market like Los Angeles that will deliver a 5% return or buy two assets in tier-two markets at a blended cap rate of 6.75%.

Cap rates are a great way to compare different asset classes and different markets, but let's rewind and determine how to calculate the NOI of an investment.

NOI – NET OPERATING INCOME

The second critical metric needed to accurately value commercial real estate is NOI (net operating income).

There are two ways in which you can use NOI when calculating cap rate.

First is using the "in-place" NOI of the property. This is the trailing twelve-month NOI stated on the profit and loss statement (aka P&L statement) usually provided by the seller.

What is a property's NOI? You can find it with the following formula:

NOI = Effective Gross Income (EGI) - Operating Expenses (OPEX)

EGI – EFFECTIVE GROSS INCOME

In the NOI formula, EGI is the gross potential rent (GPR) you'd receive if your property was full and rented at market rents minus rental losses.

Most property managers would love having a fully rented property with renters paying the exact market rates. Unfortunately for them, and you, these conditions are seldom met. In this regard, you can think of GPR as more of a theoretical figure. It's the "best case scenario," which is fine for our purposes in determining the NOI of potential investment properties.

Also, given its dependence on market rents, EGI won't be the same wherever you go. It's going to vary from one market to the next.

Mathematically, you would compute EGI like so:

EGI = Gross Potential Income - Rental Losses + Other Income

More formulas, right? It seems like I just keep throwing them at you, doesn't it? Well, I am an engineer and I love formulas! And each formula has a formula inside of it. And then a formula inside of that one too. Almost like those little Russian nesting dolls.

Fortunately, we're about done with our ever-expanding array of formulas. There are a few more coming, but when we get to those, it won't feel like we're opening a "can of worms" for each one.

Back to EGI. As you review the formula, you may be curious about *rental losses*. What are they?... Simply put, rental losses are the amount of money an investment loses as renters move in and out of your property.

The common types of rental losses are:

- Vacancy
- Bad debt
- Concessions
- Loss to lease

Since rental losses mean an investment isn't maximizing its income (aka lost revenue), it's important to understand exactly what they are and understand that this is part of owning real estate. Let's "crack open" the common rental losses on our list.

VACANCY

Vacancy, in plain English, is the number of units not rented in a given month.

Vacancy can be a huge headache if it happens too often. My first property in upstate New York had this problem. Two of the three units in the property sat vacant for an average of two to three months per year. I hadn't accounted for this level of vacancy, so my cash flow was less than I had expected.

My mistake doesn't have to be yours, though. You can accurately account for vacancy. To do that, estimate what percent of the units at your property won't be rented in any given month throughout the year. This percent is called the "vacancy percentage." You apply it to the gross income on your property, so as to reduce that income due to the empty, non-rented units. With a vacancy percent applied, you can realistically see how much you might expect to lose on vacancies.

Vacancies often fluctuate from month to month. For simplicity, just average it out.

As an example, let's say 5% of your units will not be rented each month. If you are considering purchasing a 100-unit building, 5% means five units won't be rented in any given month. That means you lose out on potential rent money and will have a reduction in your GPR.

In the example, if each unit was rented at $600, five empty units translates to $3,000 a month in rental loss (5 X $600/unit). And that's just in a month. Over a year, it amounts to $36,000 in lost money from vacancies.

Losing $36K from units lying vacant isn't fun. It is, however, something you must expect when investing in real estate. In order to make sure you are using the right assumption for vacancy, look at the trailing twelve-month P&L (profit and loss statement) to get a sense of the "in-place" vacancy. Depending on the asset, a 5% vacancy may not be a correct assumption. If a property has an in-place vacancy of 9% then your assumption should be at least 9%. Still, it's not the only percentage you could use.

◆ Rule of Thumb: When estimating vacancies, take the highest value of three possible scenarios:

1. 5% vacancy - Use this percent as a minimum

2. The current vacancy percent for the property (i.e., right now)

3. The average vacancy for the market. Compare other similar properties within a close proximity to determine the "market vacancy." Data on different markets can be found at reis.com, costar.com, or by talking to a local property manager.

As an investor, it is your job to assess what is a realistic vacancy of the potential investment. Other factors may be contributing to the fact that the in-place vacancy is higher than, say, the market average. This is a good sign for you as the investor because it indicates that the property may be run inefficiently, and you can change that by employing a professional property management team to reduce vacancies and align more with the market average.

BAD DEBT

Bad debt is another common type of rental loss, another of the "thieves" that steal your rental income. I say "thieves" figuratively but that might be a mistake. The reason is that bad debt comes from actual people. It's when tenants aren't paying their rent on time, or at all. Are these people thieves? You can decide for yourself. Just make sure you're aware of how much rental income tenants are "stealing" from you. Or rather, to be more polite about it, how much "bad debt" the property has.

Given that it's a rental loss, you'll need to determine what bad debt (if any) exists *before* you buy a property. Nothing is more distressing than investing in a property and then finding out later that you've got *bad debt*. It's like getting dressed up on Friday night, heading out with friends to a great restaurant, and finding that it's out of business. Makes for a great evening, doesn't it? Actually, it doesn't. At least with the closed restaurant, you're only temporarily hungry. With bad debt you're likely to be "hungry" for far longer and you can't just drive to another restaurant.

What you can do, though, is to accurately identify bad debt prior to a purchase. Bad debt will show up when you look at a property's *rent roll*. The *rent roll* is a full record of all the tenants renting in a building. In the *rent roll*, you'll see important rent-related details, including who's paid their rent, how much they've paid, and what their rental deposit was. All of this information will help you, the investor, understand the extent of your rental income, should you invest in a given property.

If you review a rent roll and find that most, or even all, of a property's tenants are up-to-date on their rents, it's a great sign. If, on the other hand, your perusal of the rent roll reveals a high number of tenants who are behind on their rent, you may want to think twice before investing in the property.

That said, the issue of tenants not paying rent is not necessarily the end of the world for you as an investor. You could solve it rather quickly in fact by evicting those who haven't paid. The question, though, is whether you want to go through that. And whether you then want to face the prospect of being without potential rent payments, since you'd then have vacant units. Maybe all that is fine by you, but it does need to be considered. And these considerations come from reviewing a rent roll.

As for the rent roll itself—the actual document—you may not have access to it when you're first analyzing a property. Often, for example, you'll be dealing with a "Mom and Pop" style property. Such a property would likely be owned by a couple or a family, and it probably has well under 50 units.

Given the size of the property and the background of the owners, you may not be able to get the rent rolls from the owners as a first pass. Chances are, "Mom and Pop" aren't particularly interested in giving that kind of sensitive information out to just anyone. Eventually, they do need to give you the rent rolls. But in the early stage, if the property is small, you can rely on online resources like Rentometer. com.

Getting the rent roll is done through your broker. Or if you're dealing directly with the owners, just ask them.

Another point on rent rolls: make sure you look carefully at the move-in dates of tenants. Sometimes a property's owners will fill their units with low renters to make the vacancy look better. Typically, though, these tenants only intend to stay short term and might not actually be paying rent. This is why it's important to follow your review of rent rolls with a look at all tenancy agreements. Tenancy agreements will clarify any confusion from the rent rolls and provide you with a complete picture of all renters at a property.

CONCESSIONS/LOSS TO LEASE

How else can you have a rental loss? With concessions or a loss to lease. I've grouped these last two forms of rental loss together because they're similar.

In general, concessions are a financial incentive used to induce more people to rent units in your building. You might offer prospective tenants a reduced rent, such as one month free for signing a twelve-month lease. This would be a great deal for the tenants, as they enjoy a rent-free month. Their enjoyment would come at your expense, however, since this particular concession would commit you to an entire month without income from one of your units. An entire month in which you'd have a rental loss.

If you think concessions are bad, would you prefer a loss to lease? This form of rental loss is the amount of rent that is below the overall market rent.

Let's make this clearer with an illustration. Suppose you offered tenants a $25/month reduction in rent if they stay for another year. Your loss to lease would therefore be $25 x 12 months, since that's the reduced amount from tenants.

Another good example is when market rents increase during a twelve-month period. Say you sign up a tenant at $600/month, which at the time is "market rent." Over the next six months, however, market rents increase to $625/month. Assuming market rents don't increase any further, you now have a $25/month loss to lease. Your loss to lease will persist for the next six months until the end of the current tenancy agreement. Once the agreement has ended, you can then renegotiate a higher price to match the new market rent. Until that point, though, you're saddled with the $25/month loss.

Depressed thinking about rental losses? Then you'll be delighted to know that rental losses aren't all doom and gloom. Rental losses and lost revenue are a fact of life, a byproduct of operating any business. They can be minimized, or even reduced, through better property management. Moreover, your properties can be made even more profitable than at present. One of the best ways to accomplish this is through "other income."

OTHER INCOME

Like the name suggests, "other income" consists of other sources of income (revenue) that you can generate from your property. What are those other sources, exactly? That's where the fun begins. You, as an investor, get to find and/or create the other sources of income. And there's virtually no limit to the number of sources or the amount of income you can generate.

Naturally, you don't want to approach this in a way that's petty or greedy. I'm not recommending, for example, that you begin charging tenants for normal usage of your building's elevator, a move that could also lose you tenants fast, perhaps at the rate of an elevator ride—two floors per minute.

Instead of charging for things like elevator use, I recommend thinking of logical, justifiable sources of "other income." Below is a list of common sources to help you get started. All of the sources on the list are ways you can potentially increase the NOI and the value of your property. Whether you're able to apply them depends on your individual property and whether your tenants are willing to pay.

Common sources of other income:

- Application fees - These are fees a tenant pays when they first sign a lease.

- Late fees on rent - What a client pays you if their rent is late. As a caution, make sure to always have late fees written into your rental agreement. An example of late fees would be tenants agreeing to pay a $50 penalty if they haven't given you rent by the tenth of the month.

- Parking fees - charging tenants for assigned or covered parking.

- Pet fees - charging tenants for having pets like a dog or cat.

- Washer/dryer income - This income can be collected by having a coin laundry on-site. Or you can get it by supplying washers/dryers in the units at an additional monthly charge, on top of rent. Both options work well if implemented correctly.

- Utility Fees/RUBS - Here, you're billing back tenants for usage of utilities (e.g., water, gas, electricity) if the property isn't individually metered.

- Month-to-month rental premiums.

- Key fees/deposits - Keys can be a key to other income. With a key fee or deposit, fees are charged when tenants take the keys at the beginning of the lease. You do this as a safeguard against future break-ins or key-related issues.

- Club house rental - If you have a clubhouse on your property, put it to good use by charging tenants to rent it.

Got all that? Not just the list of other income sources. I'm talking about everything else we've covered in this chapter. All the formulas and jargon. It may seem heavy, but we're almost through.

So, we've covered effective gross income (EGI). With that in our rear-view mirror, let's look at operating expenses (OPEX). Operating expenses were, if you'll recall, the second part of our formula for finding the net operating income (NOI) of a rental property. In case you've forgotten NOI's formula, here it is again:

NOI = Effective Gross Income (EGI) - Operating Expenses (OPEX)

We're done with the first part, EGI. Yet, as the formula indicates EGI doesn't give you the full story on NOI. You've also got to account for operating expenses by subtracting them out. Let's cover OPEX and see what it entails.

OPEX - OPERATING EXPENSES

Operating expenses are the expenses you incur as an investor in owning your rental property.

These expenses will vary slightly, depending on which asset class you invest in. For the sake of simplicity, let's just focus on residential assets (multifamily).

For these kinds of assets, operating expenses typically include:

- Property insurance
- Property taxes
- Repairs and maintenance
- Utilities
- Property management fees

Property taxes and insurance vary across the US. To get a good handle on what you'll spend on either, I recommend talking to the current property owners. You can also look online (with Google) or call a local insurance agency and ask for a quote. Your local city government might even be able to provide you with an approximate percentage of the property value (for taxes).

In these latter two cases (agencies and the city government), make sure everyone you talk to is familiar with the type of asset you're buying. This way they can provide you with the most accurate and relevant advice.

While you're at it, be sure your efforts also include building quality relationships with local property managers. They'll provide you with a wealth of knowledge about your local market, including information on the associated costs for utilities, repairs maintenance, and property fees.

Not a people person? Bad at building relationships with strangers? Don't worry, you're not alone. As an engineer and a "math guy," I can certainly feel your pain. My prescription for overcoming the "pain" is to first remember why you're doing this. Recall the 9 to 5 drudgery and your desire to break free. Think too about passive income and how incredible you *will* feel when your money is working for you, 24 hours a day.

Once you're clear on why, roll up your sleeves and start calling or emailing people to build relationships. You'll probably have some awkward calls, where you're unsure of what to say. Your emails too will probably not be "perfect" and many may go unanswered. But it really doesn't matter. What matters is that you've taken action. You've moved beyond the "someday" stage and you're actually reaching out to property managers, brokers, and others to obtain valuable information and create lasting relationships.

As you form connections, you'll gain more knowledge about a property's OPEX and be able to assess NOI.

Here's an example of how you'd find NOI.

For ease of understanding, I've split out the individual items in this NOI calculation. They are as follows:

1. Take a 50-unit property, for which the purchase price is $2,500,000.

2. Assume all of the units have two bedrooms.

3. Your average rental income on each unit would be $600/month.

> Note: We'd find this using our old friend Rentometer.com. Rentometer was the site I mentioned at the end of Chapter 2, in the comfort challenge. (You did do the comfort challenge, didn't you?)

With Rentometer's help, you can get a good feel for the average rental prices within a one- to two-mile radius of any property you're considering.

1. Your gross income from the 50-unit property would be $30,000/month (50 units X $600/month/unit).

2. The gross income must take vacancies into account. With our default percent of 5%, vacancies come out to $1,500/month. ($30,000/month X 0.05).

3. Subtract vacancies from the gross income. The new gross income, accounting for vacancies, comes out to $28,500/month. ($30,000/month, minus, $1,500/month).

4. Vacancies aren't the only thing for us to subtract. We've also got to remove operating expenses: OPEX. For this example, we'll say OPEX is $13,500/month.

5. We now subtract the OPEX from the EGI to arrive at our NOI (net operating income) for the property. The NOI works out to be $15,000/month. ($28,500/month EGI minus $13,500/

month OPEX).

6. Annually our NOI is $180,000 ($15,000/month X 12 months).

Building on this example, with its NOI, we can now calculate two other important figures. These are cap rate and cash flow.

For cap rate, recall how it was determined. We got it through dividing annual NOI by the property's price. In our example, we'd get a cap rate of 7.2%. ($180,000 annual NOI, divided by the $2,500,000 property price).

That's the cap rate. How about cash flow? What would that work out to?

CASH FLOW

Mathematically, we'd start on cash flow with an understanding of the following formula:

Cash Flow = NOI - Debt Services

Debt services are defined as mortgage payments on the debt used to purchase the property.

For simplicity with debt services, let's use the following information:

- 5% interest rate on the debt
- Amortized over 25 years
- A down payment of 25% is required to purchase the property. Thus, our down payment is $625,500 (0.25 X $2,500,000 property price)
- Our financed amount (the debt) is $1,875,000 ($2,500,000 property price minus $625,000 down payment)

Armed with these stats, you can calculate the monthly mortgage payments. If you instinctively know how to do that, great! If not, just go to Google and search "mortgage calculator."

Run the numbers and you'll find that your monthly mortgage payment, in our example, is $10,065.

Thus, we arrive at long last, upon the most important item in all of these calculations. We finally have a basis to know our cash flow— what we get to keep at the end of the day. It is the amount that comes to us in passive income and can stay in our bank account for personal use.

In the above example, the monthly cash flow equals $4,935. ($15,000/ month NOI, minus, $10,065/month mortgage payments).

Over the course of a year, our $4,935 monthly cash flow equates to $52,220. ($4,935 X 12 months).

$52,220 per year? That's a comfortable salary for many people. Imagine what your own life could be like by earning a year's salary while you sleep. This premise of a "salary while asleep" should, ironically, keep you up at night. If nothing else, it should help you recognize more clearly the potential of REI.

To further illustrate REI's potential, let's continue on with our example.

We can find out, for instance, whether you're better off buying the hypothetical property or buying stocks. We learn that through calculating your cash-on-cash return (CoC return).

CASH-ON-CASH RETURN

The cash-on-cash (CoC) return is the ratio of your cash flow divided by your down payment.

With our long-running example, the CoC return would be 8.35%. We'd arrive at this percent by dividing our $52,220 annual cash flow, by the $625,000 down payment (25% of the total purchase price of $2,500,000).

You'd get an 8.35% return from investing in real estate in this example. Does your current stock portfolio produce that type of return? What about your bank CD, whose interest payments are so tiny that you have to squint to see the extra cents you've earned?

We both know the answers to these questions. It's a firm "NO" in both cases. Your stocks aren't going to give you an 8.35% return and neither is the bank. Not unless you're Warren Buffet, perhaps, or have a cool million already in the bank. My guess, however, is that you're neither of these. At least when you're awake and not off in "dreamland."

This return from investing in real estate also doesn't take into account the taxation benefits from owning hard assets: the IRS gives you fantastic tax breaks for providing housing. Because the government isn't in the business of providing housing, they want to incentivize investors with great tax benefits.

REI's CoC return also beats stocks and bank interest for another important reason. Unlike either of those, you can raise the amount of your return by increasing the gross income and changing the value of the property.

Look at that with some data and you'll see the potential. The numbers really don't lie. Using our ongoing example, suppose we can increase the gross income by $2,000 a month. We'd do it, let's say, by increasing rents. Or, we might implement one of those "other income" strategies discussed earlier in the chapter, like charging a pet fee or adding laundry facilities.

How do these actions change the value of the property?

The property's value increases, and it works like this:

1. The gross income for your property increases by $2,000 from its previous amount ($30,000) to the new amount of $32,000.

2. All that's changed is the gross income, so vacancy and expenses stay the same at $15,000.

3. Doing an NOI calculation, we find that it's $17,000. ($32,000 EGI minus $15,000 OPEX)

4. The new property value is now determined by taking our new NOI ($17,000) and making it an annual NOI. ($17,000 NOI/ month X 12 months)

5. After getting a new annual NOI ($204,000), we then divide it by the cap rate from earlier (7.2%). This gives us the new value of the property, $2,833,333. ($204,000 annual NOI, divided by, 0.072 for cap rate)

At its new value ($2,833,333), your property has come a considerable distance from where it was before ($2,500,000). Quite a way, in fact. Like $333,333! All because you did something as simple as increasing rents, or adding a pet fee, or installing a laundry facility.

Exciting isn't it, the thought of what you can accomplish with changes like that? But it also illustrates the importance of control in your investment. You as the investors can "control" your investments, unlike when you invest in the stock market.

CURB YOUR ENTHUSIASM... OVER REI

Still, don't let your excitement blind you. Excitement alone isn't enough to succeed in REI. You also need to be fully knowledgeable about it.

Being knowledgeable in REI means you must understand that each of your properties is a business. As such, you need to treat the properties as you would any other business. Meaning you're constantly watching the numbers so you'll spot new opportunities to make money.

The opportunities will likely present themselves in the form of NOI-increasing activities.

Recall how you can make such increases through three basic methods. You should constantly seek to maximize NOI through any and/or all of them. For those who've forgotten, those three methods are:

1. Increasing rents

2. Creating other sources of income

3. Reducing the operating expenses of the property

Also remember that NOI forces appreciation on your property. I could talk for hours about how amazing this is. And I probably have, too, on my long-running podcast, so there's no need to bore you here. Suffice it to say that, for every dollar you increase the NOI, the value of your property goes up.

By how much? That will depend on the cap rate. If, for example, you're in an area where the cap rate is 10 ("a 10-cap area"), a $1 NOI increase makes your property's value go up by $10.

Amazing isn't it? Yet for the umpteenth time, don't rush off now. Learn how REI works and do all the "legwork" up front before you ever invest in anything.

Doing that "legwork" includes, by the way, finishing this book. It'll be worthwhile, I promise. In fact, the next chapter alone might pay for the entire cost of this book. We'll be covering how to get set up for investing in real estate. Being properly set up will save you substantial money, since you'll avoid tax penalties and other costly problems.

Let's learn how, proceeding on now to Chapter 4.

COMFORT CHALLENGE

Before we head to Chapter 4, here's a comfort challenge for you. I talked before about emailing property managers and brokers, and I stressed its importance. For our comfort challenge, go one step beyond in your outreach.

Find a well-known "big deal" real estate investor in your area. Once you have this person in mind, I want you to do the *unthinkable*. The thing you might *never, ever* feel comfortable doing.

Email or call this "big deal" REI guy/gal and invite them to coffee or lunch, your treat. Make sure, though, that it's indeed your treat (i.e., you're paying!).

Think carefully, too, about what you can contribute. Make sure there's something you can add to the exchange, even if it's as simple as a willingness to help the investor you're meeting.

Finally, when the big day does come, be sure you're on time and prepared with what you want to ask of the investor. Tardiness and lack of preparation are precisely what makes some "big shot" investors cringe at the thought of a "pick your brain" session.

Deep down, most of the "big shots" really do want to share their knowledge, perhaps even mentor new investors like you. Why? Because they know what it was like to be where you are. They can relate and feel a desire to help new investors avoid all the pains they had to go through.

So don't be intimidated at the thought of contacting REI's "big shots." Many of them are already on your side. All you have to do is treat them with respect. If you can do that, you'll be amazed at the meetings you have and the connections you build. "Life-changing" might be the best way to describe your results. Go ahead, try it!

★★ AUSSIE-ISMS ★★

More Aussie-isms to add to your collection:

1. "Arvo" – Afternoon; When you might have coffee with a "big shot" investor.

2. "Togs" – A swimsuit; What you shouldn't wear when meeting the investor.

3. "Sickie" – A sick day from work; You might take one to have that coffee meeting.

4. "Smoko" – When you take a lunch break. "I am going for smoko".

CHAPTER 4

GETTING SET UP TO INVEST

"I was set up!"

Funny how that can be a very bad thing, outside of REI. We think, perhaps, of murder or framing someone for a crime.

In REI, on the other hand, you'll want to be "set up" before you start investing here in the US. The proper setup, before investing, will allow you to "make a killing" on your properties, and your cash flow will be so good, it feels almost "criminal."

How do you get set up for REI? We're going to focus on this topic in the chapter ahead. Unlike the previous chapter with all its formulas, this one is going to be much more "black and white." Our discussion will show you what's required to get set up here in the US before you start investing, and precisely how you do it.

Getting set up means that you have checked everything and done the work to fully prepare yourself—legally, financially, and in a true business sense—to do deals.

So we're clear, let me tell you right up front that I help international investors get set up. It's one of my services. You can see exactly what I provide at www.reedgoossens.com/international-investor/

You shouldn't underestimate your ability to get set up. Much of the process is easier than you'd expect. Plus, you're probably more capable than you realize.

Even if you're not feeling capable, we can change that. My goal in this chapter, like the rest of this book, is to educate and empower you so you have the keys to figuratively drive. If at that point you'd like help, feel free to reach out. But if you're on a roll yourself, "good on ya" (good job), as we Aussies say.

At any rate, let's continue in getting you set up to invest.

The first and arguably most important area to address with set up is taxation. Taxation's importance is underscored by Benjamin Franklin's statement that there are only two certainties in life—death and taxes. Taxation isn't going away any time soon, so you must plan accordingly.

"And now, let's review your self-employment schedule C form..."

CartoonStock.com

This means "wrapping your head" around the US taxation system. Naturally, that's easier said than done. It can be a real challenge to understand REI-related taxes.

Take it from me, an engineer and a "numbers guy." Even with my background, I still struggled to "get" US taxation. So I'm right there with you, the new RE investor. I understand how the US tax system can seem complicated, confusing, and expensive. Moreover, I fully understand how taxation can seem like even more of a fearsome foe for foreign investors. Trust me; I've been there too.

The important part, though, is to push through taxes, turning what seems like a stumbling block into a stepping stone. To help you do that, let's walk through how US taxes work and then discuss how you can arrange your affairs in the way that's most beneficial to you.

In talking about taxes, let me preface with an obvious disclaimer—I'm *not* a tax professional. Nor do I, as the expression goes, "play one on TV." For this reason, I've sought professional help in compiling the information here on taxes. Everything you're about to read about taxes has been vetted and partly written by trained tax professionals. Those professionals would be my good friends over at Non-Resident Tax Advisor (NRTA). They help foreign investors with their taxation needs for US investments.

NRTA has helped me with this chapter and given me greater confidence in handling US REI-related taxes. If you'd like to be more confident in your taxes as well, or you have a few questions, I'd encourage you to reach out. Contact NRTA through a special page on their website, a page that's exclusively for readers of this book. It's all waiting for you at www.reedgoossens.com/NTRA.

Proceeding now with our discussion, let's talk taxes.

In the US, you can expect to be taxed at three levels—federal, state, and local. Federal taxes are what you pay on the income you earn anywhere in the United States. No matter where in the country you're located, you'll be paying federal taxes on whatever you earn.

Curious how much you'll pay? As you might expect, it depends. Federal income taxes are based on a graduated tax system. The system uses several tax brackets to determine what taxes are owed. The brackets, in turn, depend on the type of tax entity and whether the entity is subject to certain taxes.

Along with federal taxes, you the investor also get to "enjoy" paying state and local taxes. Those types of taxes can't chase you around the country like federal taxes. Instead, state and local taxes only apply to a particular state and local jurisdiction. Because of their nature, state and local taxes vary from one area to the next.

Knowing about federal, state, and local taxes is fine on a broad level. But it doesn't address the specifics of real estate investment. This is why we need to go one step further now and examine how REI fits into the equation.

When it comes to REI, US taxes fall into three basic categories—real property taxes, capital gains, and taxable income.

REAL PROPERTY TAXES

Real property taxes are those REI-related taxes in the US that are collected at the local level. An agency in a particular location determines their own appraised value of the real property. Taxes are then imposed, based often on a percentage of the tax-appraised amount.

Since it's based on an appraisal, the value determined by a local agency often differs from other appraised values of the same property. I can't speak to your case with this. But I can help you understand, broadly, how local agencies arrive at their figures for real property taxes.

The key is to know about "*mill rate*." It's used to determine how much

you owe in taxes for one of your investments. Mill rate
to as the "*millage rate*."

In either case, we're talking about a figure representing
per $1,000 of the assessed value of the property (aka t.
fair market rate).

What's with the "mill" part? It's taken from a Latin word meaning
"thousandth," with one mill being equal to 1/1,000th of a currency
unit.

In the context of taxes, the mill rate will vary numerically from 0–4%.
It also varies from state to state, and county to county within the state.

As a personal example, one of my properties in Texas has a mill rate
of 2.65%. The resulting tax that I pay each year on the property is
2.65% multiplied by the appraised value.

To get a sense of what the mill rate would be on properties you'd
acquire, check the website of the tax agency in the county where your
properties would be located. Chances are, you'll find the mill rate on
the agency's website. With it, you can then do some easy multiplica-
tion and have an estimate of the real property taxes you'd pay.

CAPITAL GAINS

Capital gains are the second basic way you can be taxed as a real estate
investor. These taxes come if you sell real estate that you've held for
over one year (365 days) and make a profit. Your profit is considered
"capital gains" and is subject to taxes.

How much you pay in capital gains taxes is determined by comparing
the sale amount that you received to the "*adjusted basis.*" The adjusted
basis equals the original purchase price you paid plus commissions,
closing costs, and improvements to the property since the date you
bought it.

..ie last part of the adjusted basis calculation—major improvements to the property—can include expansions or major renovations. Either will raise the adjusted basis, reflecting the money you put into the improvements. Over time, though, the buildings and other man-made improvements will age and decay. For that reason, the law allows *depreciation* to lower your adjusted basis. (We've covered this before and I'll tell you more about depreciation shortly.)

Depending on what your adjusted basis ends up being, you'll be taxed accordingly. The taxes come, as we've said, if the sale price is higher than your adjusted basis. Provided that's the case, the difference is taxed as a capital gain.

While capital gains taxes can affect you, they don't necessarily have to. With a bit of cleverness, you can defer capital gains taxes.

Yes, you read that right—you can defer capital gains taxes.

To learn how, go to Chapter 11. And I'm not talking about filing for bankruptcy. That's the *other* Chapter 11. No, go to Chapter 11 of this book. There, you can read more on how to defer capital gains taxes.

**Spoiler alert: Capital gains can be deferred through buying a "like-kind" asset within 180 days of selling your existing asset. It's done via a section of the tax code called *1031 Exchange*, which we talked about earlier.

Back to capital gains taxes. If you do have to pay them, here are some other helpful points.

The rate of capital gains taxes varies, depending on how much total taxable income a person earns during the year. This goes for both real estate investments you'd personally own and those you'd own through a "flow-through entity" (to be defined soon).

As for the rates themselves, the exact capital gains rates are: 0% for lower income brackets, 15% for the next tier, and 20% for taxable income over $200,000.

Also, when your investments are based on personal, or real, property, and you've held them for under one year, your gains are taxed at ordinary graduated rates.

Understand, too, how corporations are treated on capital gains taxes. This is especially important if you've thought of forming a corporation for your REI activities. You might be even more interested in forming one now, since corporations do not receive capital gains treatment.

OK, that more than covers capital gains for our purposes here. We wanted to get a basic sense of them, and we've certainly done so. If you're still curious about capital gains, refer to Appendix [A]. There, you'll find a chart of the Federal Income Tax rates for 2018. *And as always, consult your tax professional to further understand your US tax obligations as they relate to your situation and the number of assets you own.*

TAXABLE INCOME

The last basic type of US taxes related to REI is taxable income. It becomes relevant when you own a property that produces positive cash flow. Regardless of whether the property is an apartment building or a personal residence, you're taxed on any rental income from it. The taxes you pay are determined by deducting a range of expenses including management fees, repairs/improvements, property taxes, insurance, mortgage interest, and depreciation from gross rents collected.

As you think about taxable income in greater detail, here are a few related topics to consider:

1) Depreciation

Whenever you calculate taxable income on your US rental property/ properties, make sure you consider depreciation. Deprecation helps you write off, and thereby reduce, some of your taxes.

Depreciation is based on the US government's allowance for depreciating an asset's value over its life span. Under these terms, the government's tax division—the IRS—sets the useful life of a building at 27.5 years for residential assets and 39 years for commercial assets. The IRS then views the value of a building as decreasing in a straight line from 100%, when the timer starts, down to 0%, 27.5 years later, or 39 years if you own commercial real estate.

This depreciation means your taxable income might be well below your net cash gains. In other words, only a portion of your rental income would be taxed.

Once a building is fully depreciated, however, that taxable portion will rise. So, too, will your tax payments. [**Side note: While buildings depreciate, the land value does not.]

Faced with rising payments, 27.5 years is a pivotal moment. It's a time when investors often begin thinking about selling their property and buying a new one. Will you?

You might. But then, there's no guarantee your building will even make it that far. Most buildings have lifespans well under 27.5 years. So as an investor, depreciation will probably be your friend more than your enemy, at least where taxes are concerned.

2) Passive vs. Active Income

Passive income. We want it as real estate investors. And, as it turns out, so does the IRS.

In the IRS's case, they aren't looking at passive income as a way to work less. The agency thinks about it from the standpoint of how to tax your REI income. Your income will be taxed differently, depending on whether the IRS considers it "passive" or "active" income.

In general, the income from most real estate investments is considered passive. The reason is that most real estate investments are managed by third-party property managers and not the owner(s). This is especially true for first-time investors because the average first-timer doesn't actively "work" on their properties, nor is it their trade or business.

Don't assume, though, that your REI income will automatically be seen by the IRS as passive income. It might. But then it might not.

Another way to look at *"active income"* is to be considered a *real estate professional* in the eyes of the IRS. To be a "real estate professional," a taxpayer must provide more than one-half of his or her total personal services in real property trades or businesses. The IRS defines this as spending more than *750 hours* of services during the tax year in real property trades, activities, or businesses in which you can be considered a "real estate tax professional." If you think you spend more than 750 hours a year in real-estate-related activities or businesses and you are considering being classified as a real estate professional, you should prepare contemporaneous time logs that detail the services and activities rendered.

Avoid taking a chance and consult your local tax professional to determine how actively you are involved with your real estate investments.

3) Cost Segregation (aka Accelerated Depreciation)

Then there's cost segregation. It's the practice of identifying assets and their costs, and then classifying those assets for federal tax purposes to aid with "accelerating" depreciation of an asset.

That explanation may sound vague or complex to you, so here's another way to think about it. Consider cost segregation to be "accelerated depreciation" for individual items in your investment property. On these terms, cost segregation means looking at certain costs, which have previously been classified as subject to a depreciable lifespan of either 27.5 years (for residential investments) or 39 years (for commercial investments), and classifying them as personal property or land improvements. With either classification, the items under discussion are subject to a 5-, 7-, or 15-year rate of depreciation using accelerated methods.

I realize that may still sound vague. Here then is an example of accelerated depreciation. With any luck, it'll clarify and breathe some life into cost segregation.

Our example is for a refrigerator you've purchased for the investment property. A fridge isn't going to last 27.5 years. Spam or peanut butter left in a fridge might last that long, but certainly not the refrigerator itself. For this reason, the refrigerator has a different "useful life" (lifespan) than the building it sits in. The refrigerator's "useful life" will be far less. You can accordingly depreciate it over a shorter span of time and realize the depreciation benefits sooner than the building.

Great as it is, cost segregation isn't something you can guess at. I'd like to think, for example, that a yoga mat in the fitness center of one of my buildings can be cost segregated. After all, the mat is an investment in six-pack abs. And its "lifespan" is five minutes, or the time it takes a person to sweat so much the mat becomes "unusable."

I'm joking about yoga mats "depreciating" in value. My point, though, is that like passive and active income, you shouldn't guess on cost segregation. Not only is it unwise, but it's also not the way cost segregation is handled.

To be eligible for cost segregation, the investment property must be inspected by a qualified third-party cost segregation service, or expert. The inspector performs an "engineering-based" study, which then allows a building owner to depreciate a new or existing structure and its contents in the shortest amount of time permissible under current tax laws.

Having a cost segregation study performed might sound like a lot of work. Maybe it is, but think of the benefits. We're talking serious benefits to you, the investor. Like an immediate increase in your cash flow. Or a reduction in your current tax liability. Or even getting to defer taxes.

Sweet as those benefits are, they have hidden costs. Not only does a cost segregation study take time, but you've also got to pay for it, usually $5,000–$10,000 or more, depending on the size of the property. So before you jump in and complete cost segregation, think about the overall cost benefit to your situation.

Also realize that a cost segregation study generally allows classifying 30% to 40% of the property's assets as 5-, 7-, or 15-year property. Those percentages might not sound huge, yet think of what they translate into. Completing a cost segregation on your asset increases the depreciation deduction, resulting in the deferral of a significant percentage of income taxes for the given period.

As you defer a percent of income taxes, you save. The guideline on savings is that for every $100,000 moved from 39-year to 5-year property, your initial tax savings will be $20,000 to $25,000. For savings like those, would you invest in a cost segregation study?

My question isn't rhetorical. You should think carefully about it, assessing whether a cost segregation study makes sense for your property. The investment property you own might be unsuited, for example, if it's too small. A property that's too small is one where the gross income won't be enough to pay for a cost segregation study.

This explains why cost segregation is typically used for large commercial properties where the gross income is significant enough to pay for the study. I can't speak to your particular situation, though. You need to assess it after consulting your tax advisor.

Speaking of tax advisors, here's how you can see if you're dealing with a true professional. When talking to an advisor, casually mention that you're planning to hold your real estate properties in your name. Wait for a response. Then, if the tax advisor doesn't object… run!

Why? To understand, we need to look at another part of getting set up for REI: entity selection and how it relates to asset protection from a liability and taxation point of view.

ENTITY SELECTION

There are two main reasons for not holding an asset in your name: 1) personal liability and 2) taxation liability.

Holding an REI property in your name makes you legally liable. For that reason, it's never advisable. And anyone calling themselves an advisor should know this. If they don't, or they don't care enough to tell you, move on.

What do we mean by "legally liable"? Being legally liable for an REI property means you're personally responsible for what happens to your tenants at the property. If one of your tenants, for example, falls and gets injured in the lobby, you could have a serious problem. The tenant could hold you responsible for their injury and come after you.

When they do, the injured tenant probably won't "come after you" in a literal sense. Their injury probably prevents it. Nor do you have to worry, in most cases, about the tenant sending any hit men after you either. That's the stuff of movies. Your problem instead will be that the injured tenant has filed a lawsuit against you.

With the lawsuit, your tenant is taking you, personally, to court. You're therefore the subject of the case. The court will consider, for example, what you could have done differently. And what you might provide the tenant as adequate compensation for their injury, an injury which you're liable for. You. You. You. Get the picture?

To avoid personal liability, you must have an entity. Plain and simple.

Think of an entity like a layer of protection. It's protecting you when a tenant opens fire. Your tenants can take shots at you, with lawsuits, but your personal assets, your home, and your income are safe. To ensure lawsuits can't get through the entity to hit you, make sure you consult a legal attorney to make sure you are setting up your entity in the correct way to maximize your protection.

What exactly is an entity? It's a legal structure upon which your rental property business is based. The common types of entities include a corporation, a Limited Liability Company (LLC), a Limited Partnership (LP), and a Limited Liability Partnership (LLP).

Let's consider the taxation side of the equation for entities. Of these entity types, only corporations are considered "stand-alone entities." This means a corporation's members will be responsible for filing and paying income taxes related to the corporation. In contrast, LLCs,

LPs, and LLPs are considered "flow-through entities." Being "flow-through entities" enables the people behind each of the latter three to not pay income taxes at the entity level. Instead, the member(s) or partner(s) are responsible for paying income taxes on a personal level. That is, they pay taxes for themselves as anyone—entity or not—would do.

It's worth noting that at lower income brackets, income taxes tend to be lower for individuals than corporations. Also, holding rental property in an LLC, LP, or LLP isn't without its drawbacks. Chief among the drawbacks are the additional compliance costs, especially professional fees for more income tax returns and costs associated with setting up the entity, such as state filing fees (typically paid yearly), and the associated costs of forming the legal paperwork for the entity (mainly operating agreements, articles of incorporation, etc.)

Personally, I'd say those drawbacks are worth it. In my case, I set up an LLC, RSN Property Group, LLC. Like any LLC, mine has articles of incorporation that have been filed with the state where I own property. These articles are a statement of information on the LLC and the LLC's operating agreement.

Having these documents is essential both from a legal standpoint and for staying organized. I can't emphasize the importance of those two points enough. When you form an entity, you can't do it carelessly. Otherwise, you're setting yourself up for problems. Instead, approach the matter in an organized, methodical manner.

As you do, take the time to select the type of entity that is suited to your situation, and then get the proper documentation. Make sure to maintain your LLC properly, so it's up-to-date on all filings and has enough reserves to cover debts and business affairs.

Your LLC's reserves will come from funding, and you'll state in the operating agreement how that specifically works. Also, make sure your LLC has its own separate bank account. This way, you'll be able to prove the LLC is truly separate from you.

It's also important to make sure you specify clearly when money will leave the LLC's bank account. This saves you from having profits "trapped" in the LLC bank account when they could be in your bank account.

I'm not suggesting, though, that your LLC bank account should be liquidated whenever money comes in. The LLC's bank account needs to be maintained, after all, and kept at adequate levels for running your business. My point is that you must document the times in which money will leave the LLC. You'll do that by specifying frequencies in your operating agreement. Typical frequencies for money leaving an LLC are quarterly, monthly, and yearly. These can be adjusted depending on the wishes of you and any partners in your LLC.

Lastly on LLCs, I'd encourage you to start with just one. Keep it simple, at least in the beginning. Focus on a single LLC, thereby limiting your liability to one entity. Then, if you find it makes sense to have more than one LLC, or other entity type, you can do that. You might create an LLC, for instance, that was a member of your original LLC. But that can get complicated fast. And in the beginning, it's probably unnecessary for you anyway. One entity, LLC or otherwise, is likely all you need when setting up.

While we're on entities, let me share my own story of setting up my first LLC.

Looking back, all I can say is "Wow!" Not because it was an arduous process, but because of how badly I stumbled. I jumped the gun and set up my LLC before I had even identified the property that I was going to buy. This meant paying $2,000 to have the LLC set up. The money was essentially wasted because my new LLC had nothing to protect. This is why I've stressed to you the need for taking things slowly and carefully on entities. Slow, careful movement will save you money and, if nothing else, you'll have less legal paperwork to deal with.

We're good now on entities. That's everything you need to know, at least initially, in thinking about them. We will turn now to three more areas that will be necessary for you to understand in getting set up to invest: tax withholding, money transfers, and bank accounts.

TAX WITHHOLDING

When it comes to taxes, US non-residents have all the "fun." Unlike residents, non-residents "enjoy" a mandatory 30% income tax withholding on gross rents. The withholding tax must be submitted to the IRS on a quarterly basis too.

My guess is that nearly all non-residents find these withholding requirements to be a burden. The sort of burden that can hopefully be overcome.

The key lies with ITINs. An ITIN or individual taxpayer identification number shows the IRS that you're an investor. The ITIN will be used in place of a social security number. You'll place it, for example, on the Form W-8ECI, which is given to your property manager when handling withholding. Depending on your situation, the ITIN may be used on other forms and occasions as well.

To obtain your ITIN, you should work with an IRS "Certifying Acceptance Agent." The agent will help you expedite the process of getting your ITIN and ensure you avoid any unnecessary income tax withholding.

Getting your ITIN won't be necessary, however, until after you've identified a property to invest in. At that point, you'll need an ITIN to file taxes, but not before. So, once more, don't jump the gun.

When the time does come, I'd recommend contacting one person in particular. His name is Ben Gray, and he runs a company called American Properties (www.americanproperties.com.au/). Ben and his talented team specialize in helping foreign investors with ITINS, LLCs, and other setup matters. I've had him on my podcast so you can get a sense of his background there. Here's a link to the episode: www.reedgoossens.com/tag/quit-your-day-job/page/4

Up next, let's talk about money transfers and bank accounts.

MONEY TRANSFERS AND BANK ACCOUNTS

When I say, "moving money overseas," what do you think of? Early on, my mind used to conjure up two images, one exciting and one confusing.

On the exciting side, I envisioned secret agents, with cash hidden in suitcases. They carried these suitcases through airports and narrowly avoided the border guards.

Then, on the confusing side, I envisioned stacks of paperwork as high as Australia's Ayers Rock. At 836 meters, Ayers Rock is one massive natural wonder. And I envisioned the paperwork and process of legally *"moving money overseas"* to be similarly massive in scope.

The good news is that I was wrong. Wrong on both counts. For better or worse, money transfers from one country to another lack both pulse-pounding excitement and confusion. I suppose that's a bit of a letdown if you were hoping to be like James Bond carrying suitcases of cash. Jokes aside, I think you'll be happy to know how clear the process of transferring money can be.

Note: This section is primarily aimed at foreign investors looking to get started in the US. If you're a US Citizen, you can either: 1) Skip it, going to the next section in this chapter, or 2) Read through the section and get a unique perspective that could be advantageous in your future investing career. Personally, I recommend #2, but it's your call, and we can still be friends either way.

Let's start by addressing why you even need to transfer money. Can't you just use traveler's checks or go to the ATM?

No. No. Those methods may work when you're on vacation in the US, but neither is suitable for the larger and more serious matters of investing in US real estate. Picture going to the ATM for that and it's practically laughable. Laughable to you, and certainly laughable in the eyes of anyone you'd be buying property from or investing with as a partner.

In place of such silliness, you need to engage in money transfers, or foreign exchange trades. Transferring in the sense of moving your money out of your country and having the money in US dollars. This way, you have cash on hand to use in purchasing your real estate investments.

Given the importance of money transfers, there are a host of services out there to aid you. Of these, I've chosen World First to handle my money transfers. They handle money transfers for investors worldwide.

Reach out to www.worldfirst.com to find out more about how they can help you easily and safely transfer your money into USD at better rates than bank-to-bank transfers.

In helping you with your transfer, World First and comparable services usually work as follows.

First, you open an account with them, usually free and with no obligation to transfer any money. With the account set up, you'll do a domestic transfer, in your home country's currency, into your account with the transfer service.

Once the money is sitting in your account, it needs to be changed into US dollars. To do that, you'll lock in a specific exchange rate for the conversion. The money transfer service will then convert the money at that agreed-upon rate. On conversion, the money in USD will be wired to whatever account you need it in. The account may be an escrow account, a bank account, or some other type. Usually, the money is wired the same day, so you can rock-n-roll and close the deal without delay.

Money transfers rock, yet you need to be aware of the requirements on them. Otherwise, you could end up between a "rock and a hard place." For requirements, know that the money you transfer needs to come from *your* account or any accounts linked to it. Also, and this is probably most important, you need to be transparent. Meaning you have to show the source of the money. This is to avoid allegations of money laundering.

Assuming you can meet these requirements, you'll be able to transfer money to your heart's content. The process I've outlined usually works in reverse too. So your rental property income, for example, can be converted from USD to your country's currency and moved to your bank account back home.

While we're on bank accounts, let's cover your options. It really comes down to two. Your first option is to have a standard US bank account. It's not impossible, but there are a lot of requirements. The largest of those is that, by law, you have to physically be in the US when setting up your bank account. That requirement could be a drawback if you're unable, or unwilling, to go to the US.

Your other option would be to use a money transfer service in place of a US bank account. Some transfer services can perform essentially the same function, as we saw earlier when covering transfer steps. However, when it's all said and done, it is advisable to travel to the US (on your next vacation) to set up your US bank account. This will simplify everything moving forward. Without a bank account to send and receive money, it makes it difficult to do business in the US.

ANOTHER SETUP

With money transfers and bank accounts done, we're at the end of our discussion on getting set up to invest in real estate. Let's close our discussion on setup by setting up the next chapter (Chapter 5).

In Chapter 5, you'll find the answer to one of the biggest questions in REI. It's a question you've undoubtedly asked yourself too. What's the question? And, just as important, what's the answer to it? All will be revealed to you in Chapter 5.

COMFORT CHALLENGE

Your comfort challenge for this chapter isn't complicated. In fact, I've just spent the entire chapter explaining it.

What's the challenge? Do what's been outlined here and get yourself set up to invest in US real estate.

★★ AUSSIE-ISMS ★★

Feeling Australian yet? If not, these slang terms should help.

1. "Give someone a bell" – Call someone on the phone; What you'll do when scheduling a meeting with a tax advisor.

2. "Uni" — University; Where you hope your tax advisor has graduated from.

3. "Bludger" — A lazy person or a loafer; A person sure to fail when investing in real estate and trying to leave the "rat race."

CHAPTER 5

FINDING THE RIGHT US MARKET TO INVEST IN

How safe do you feel walking in some neighborhoods?

Now there's a "cheerful" question. It's an important one too. It's not the question we alluded to in the last chapter.

Why mention it here? Because it's still of prime concern. Or at least it was to me.

To give you some context and explain the connection to REI, let me share a story. You'll find that it serves as a useful reference for our discussions in this chapter.

Our story begins on a sunny September morning.

On that fine day, I awoke at 5 AM with a sense of excitement. This excitement only intensified as I left my apartment and headed for NYC's Port Authority Bus Terminal.

Frankly, I felt giddy. Like I was about to cash in a winning lottery ticket.

Rather than cashing in a ticket, though, I had to take a bus trip.

And a long one at that. Nearly four hours each way, from NYC to Baltimore, Maryland.

Why Baltimore? Because it seemed like a happening place, at least from an REI standpoint. Looking online, I'd seen houses in Baltimore that you could buy for just $15,000. Not $150,000. No, just $15K.

In those days, as an aspiring real estate investor, $15K was within my price range. I'd saved the money and could now potentially buy one of these properties.

Four hours into the trip, we finally arrived in Baltimore. It was time to visit a few properties and potentially buy my first one.

Or was it?

Looking back, I can only cringe at what happened next. As we toured the various houses, it became painfully obvious to me why they were so cheap. I'd expected the houses to require some fixing up. It comes with the territory when buying low-cost properties. The amount of work required to make these places livable and appealing to renters would have likely proven exorbitantly expensive. Besides that, the houses also had two major problems that renovations couldn't fix.

The first of those problems presented itself in the form of a syringe needle. I found the needle lying discarded inside one of the vacant houses, indicating the place was an ex-drug den. Seeing the needle, I knew that this house/neighborhood had a serious drug problem. One that I didn't want to be involved with for my first purchase.

The other houses on our tour likely had similar drug issues and were all vacant. Rows and rows of houses were vacant and boarded up. Even if a house was drug-free, there was still the problem of crime. Crime, for example, by those who supplied the drug users. Crime as well, from the drug users themselves. As cheap as these houses were, this tour gave me a firsthand lesson in understanding that it would take a lot more than buying one of these houses to transition the entire neighborhood. I would have had to buy the entire block, and then work for years to help the neighborhood become a place where responsible job-holders and families would feel comfortable living. The neighborhood needed social, political, and economic investment, not just real estate investment. I'm all for lifting communities out of poverty, and sometimes it takes real estate innovation to do that. But for my purposes, this neighborhood just wasn't the right opportunity.

As the trip concluded, I knew that I would never let this happen again. Never again would I consider a property without a full understanding of its location, the local market, and the rental demographic.

Writing this now, I want to help you follow suit. Accordingly, this chapter will focus on how to find the best US markets to invest in for real estate purposes, markets that will show a return in a shorter amount of time than it would have taken to get that Baltimore neighborhood on better socioeconomic footing.

SETTING CRITERIA

When it comes to finding an ideal market, the key is to know what you're looking for. This means having tangible things in mind that indicate one market's superiority to another.

Over your career as an investor, you'll undoubtedly develop your list of things to assess. Until then, you can get started by looking over my shoulder. I'll show you in this chapter what I look for when finding great markets to invest in. What's more, I'll explain how I developed my market criteria.

My criteria are specific to investing in multifamily properties, but you'll be delighted to know they are also broad enough to apply in any asset class you're considering. So you can still rely on them, even if you'd rather invest in a different asset like self-storage, warehouses, mobile home parks, or single-family houses.

As this is my criteria, it only fits that I repeat some related advice. It's a common saying in REI, and one that I live by. *"You make money when you buy, and not when you sell!"*

Note the italics. I use them around the quote because I want you to remember it.

If those italics aren't enough, let me repeat:

"You make money when you buy, and not when you sell!"

I personally believe this saying is the most important one to live by when purchasing real estate. I consider it myself whenever I'm analyzing a deal.

With the saying, comes a natural question—how do you ensure you're buying in a money-making way?

The answer is that "it's complicated." There are a lot of factors and parameters that determine if the deal is indeed a cracker, or if it's a dud. Still, among everything, the first and most important factor lies in choosing the right US market to invest in.

Before we get into the criteria I promised, there's one more thing you should know. It'll help you to make sense of the criteria I'll be providing.

THE TRUTH ABOUT THE "US HOUSING MARKET"

What you should know is that there is no "US housing market," despite what you've heard on the news.

Newscasters can throw the term around more than a local footy team throws back stubbies after a big win, but it doesn't change the reality. Again, there is no general "US housing market." Not in that kind of uniform blanket way. What we have instead is an ultra-fragmented spread of approximately 400 metropolitan statistical areas (MSAs).

Each MSA, in turn, contains submarkets. Within each submarket, there are then suburbs. And within each suburb, there are streets. See the complexity? And it doesn't end there, either.

You've also got to think in terms of your location compared to a particular street. Being north, south, east, or west of a given street will dictate a host of things, from cap rates to rents to school districts and much more.

Can you see now why it's a mistake to refer to a generalized "US housing market"? It doesn't exist. Avoid this error and recognize the complexity. As an engineer I love complexity and diving into the weeds of a given market—learning about a given market's intricacies, where the "Path of Progress" is, where development is occurring, where major shopping centers are popping up, and much more.

Don't let the complexity intimidate you. Yes, there's a ton to consider. No denying that. But why not view it in a positive light? Rather than feeling overwhelmed by MSAs, submarkets, suburbs, and everything else, I recommend delighting in how many opportunities exist. Reframe the situation, looking at things in more appetizing terms.

AN REI "BUFFET"

I say "appetizing" because metaphorically, all the choices (MSAs, submarkets, etc.) can be likened to a buffet. Imagine a buffet that stretches for 2,680 miles (America's width). Think of all the tasty dishes you'd find on that buffet. You'd likely see everything from French fries to French foie gras; Chicken tikka masala to chicken soup; Spaghetti Bolognese to bowls of Soba noodles. And so on. Dish after dish, after dish... after dish.

Getting hungry yet? It's equally mouthwatering when you consider all the choices available to investors in US real estate. Still, if we continue our buffet metaphor, a definite problem emerges.

The problem is that, as with a large buffet, you probably can't "eat" everything. You may want to, of course. But chances are you don't have the stomach for it.

At the food buffet, if you ignore your stomach's limit and overeat, you'll get indigestion or worse. The same holds for REI. In the REI sense, you don't have the "stomach," financially, to "eat" everything you see on this figurative "buffet."

As an investor, you can certainly "sample" those properties and investment opportunities that look appetizing. In the investor case, "sampling" could mean visiting certain properties or running the numbers on various deals. Even with "sampling," though, you're still limited, both by time and available resources.

How then are you to approach this massive opportunity"? That's where those criteria I keep promising come in. With the criteria, it's like you're taking stock of the buffet overall, and then choosing to "fill your plate" (or your portfolio) with "dishes" from specific sections of the overall buffet.

The final point is that you shouldn't let geographical distance damper your excitement. I'm speaking to my international investing friends now. If you're reading this from outside the US, don't think that your distance from the market is an insurmountable obstacle. It isn't. If anything, I'd argue that being removed from the markets can empower you. The perk is that it forces you to sharpen your research and analytical skills. It's like how blindness or deafness sharpens a person's other physical senses. Being outside the US can do the equivalent for you, sharpening your senses as an investor through alternate means.

Wherever you are, geographically, you're probably foaming at the mouth now—figuratively—for those criteria for choosing the "right" US market for REI. Without further ado, here they are, in four easily-digestible steps.

STEP 1: UNDERSTAND THE DIFFERENT TYPES OF MARKETS

Your first step in selecting a market for RE investing is to understand the types of markets. This means classifying real estate markets with respect to how those markets behave. When you do, you'll find that there are three types of markets in the US: linear, cyclical, and hybrid.

Linear markets are those that appreciate steadily (typically 1–3% every year) in line with standard inflation. Cap rates in these markets are moderate, between 5% and 8%, which makes them ideal properties for cash flow, rather than a quick appreciation payday. Geographically, such markets tend to be located in America's Midwestern and southern states, cities, for example, like Kansas City, MO, Indianapolis, IN, and Raleigh, NC.

Don't forget about Texas either. The "Lone Star State" has numerous linear markets. In the case of Texas, examples of linear markets are the cities of San Antonio, Dallas-Fort Worth, and Houston.

I mention Texas, in particular, because of my own experiences there. I've personally invested in two properties within the Dallas area. While I won't bore you with financial details, let's say the returns on both properties have been excellent. So I can personally vouch for buying properties in a linear market, like the ones you'll find in Texas.

Linear markets can be great, yet don't be equally linear in your thinking. Consider other types of markets too. Like cyclical markets. Those are the second of our behavior-based market types.

Conceptually, cyclical markets behave like roller coasters, swinging sharply up and down. This behavior makes these markets good for appreciation (yearly appreciation can be up to 10% growth). The downside is that cyclical markets have high property prices. Thus, you'll usually have a difficult time finding cash flow deals in cyclical markets. Location-wise, you can find examples of these markets in America's coastal areas. Cyclical markets are present, for example, in coastal cities like San Francisco, Los Angeles, New York, and Miami.

Then there are hybrid markets. As you might guess from their name, these markets are a combination of linear and cyclical. On the linear side, a hybrid market will have a history of steady, predictable appreciation. The market has also begun, usually in recent years, to display cyclical behavior. That behavior is a result of changing employers, jobs in the market, and demographics. Those changes cause the market's population to grow at a healthy rate. Geographically, you can see cases of hybrid markets in the US cities of Austin, TX, Boulder, CO, and Charlotte, NC.

Among those cities, Austin and Boulder in particular have grown in large part due to the tech industry. While I wouldn't advise you to only consider places where tech and tech-related start-ups are strong, it does warrant some consideration. How much consideration? Hold that thought. We'll be addressing tech and other industry types in the next step.

Before we go on to that next step in choosing the "right" market for REI, I want to remind you of something. Think back to Chapter 2. Remember how we emphasized knowing your goals as an investor?

Make sure you keep those goals in mind as you're choosing a market. Your goals would help in this first step, for example, if you were having trouble deciding between two markets, one linear and the other cyclical. Thinking about your investment goals would make such a decision easier since you'd be making it in alignment with what you truly want.

STEP 2: MARKET IDENTIFICATION AND CRITERIA

Our first step was macroscopic, looking at markets from a kind of "20,000-foot view." The kind of view that daredevil Felix Baumgartner had on his record-setting jump from the stratosphere back in 2012.

Let's zoom in now, getting more "down-to-earth" in Step 2. That means looking at specific numbers. The numbers we'll now cover are at the core of my criteria for choosing a market. For these numbers to make any sense, we need to look at them as they relate to several key factors. Each factor is a litmus test, so to speak, for judging where you can invest. They are as follows:

#1 - Population

Ever heard of Key Biscayne? It's a beautiful beach town in Florida's island cluster, the Keys.

Despite the idyllic beaches, Key Biscayne is not an ideal place for REI. Not with its population, which numbers just 12,500. For tourists and residents, a population of that size is fine. For us investors, however, the population is way too small.

Ideally, I recommend considering areas with a population of at least 350,000 or more in the MSA. A population of this size will ensure reliable, long-term growth in the area. Anything smaller and the market is likely to be more susceptible to market fluctuations.

#2 - Jobs

Any area that you seriously consider for REI should have an economy based on at least three different industries. A three-industry minimum ensures your investments will fair relatively well in a downturn, even if one of the area's main industries collapses. In that case, the industry and its employers will be the only ones out of business. You the investor will still be "in business" because of the two or more other industries supporting the local economy.

I say "industries" because those are the sources of jobs. Look for the industries, and you'll find the jobs. And with the jobs, you'll find a population that's willing and able to live in your investment properties; people always need a roof over their heads.

Given their importance, you're probably wondering whether there are "good" and "bad" industries. Apart from the "world's oldest profession" (you know…hunting), I'd say there aren't "bad" industries *per se*. But if we take things purely from an investment standpoint, the overwhelming majority of industries can be considered "good."

Among the best of the bunch are restaurants, financial services and banking, tech start-ups, and technology. Any of these will help an area's population to grow steadily over time. These industries are creating jobs that attract people to migrate into the area for work.

These newcomers will need a place to live, and you, the real estate investor, can provide it.

I would steer clear of MSAs with a high proportion of employees working in one predominant sector over the others; for example, the oil and gas industry, or tourism. Both industries can fluctuate and are affected by external factors. During the 2008 financial crash, a lot of oil and gas MSAs were hit hard. In areas where oil and gas are the major employers, when jobs dry up, and there are no other industries to "pick up the slack," people tend to move to markets with more stable jobs and job creation. Keep this in mind when choosing a suitable US market to invest in.

#3 - Moderate Cap Rates

Want strong annual returns on your investment(s)? Then you need an area where the cap rates are above 5%. That's the key to great returns and a reliable cash flow.

In case you have forgotten the definition of cap rates, the term refers to how a bank values your asset over time. Cap rates are also the measure of risk and an indicator of your return on capital if you purchased a building with all-cash.

Where cap rates are concerned, keep them above 5%. You may, for example, be able to find sub markets within a certain MSA with +8% cap rates. It's perfectly feasible if the economics of a metro area are strong and the cap rates of local "Class B" properties are above 5.5%. (**Class B properties are those buildings constructed in the 1980s and 1990s. For a full discussion on all the property classes, stay tuned!)

#4 - Multifamily Occupancy Trends

Multifamily occupancy trends are another of our factors to consider. Specifically, you'll want to look for MSAs where the average occupancy for multifamily buildings is 90% or more. Anything north of 90% is "healthy" because it signals a growing population that's outpacing the current supply of new apartments.

At the same time, though, keep in mind that there can be exceptions. You may, for example, find a property within a market that's been mismanaged. If "Mom and Pop" are running the place, perhaps their focus hasn't been on filling the building with renters. In this case, the occupancy may have slipped. This would create an excellent opportunity for you, as an investor, to then purchase the property, add value by increasing the number of tenants, and be rewarded.

Also, as you think about trends in multifamily, it's important to consider a big one. It's a trend I'm keenly aware of while writing this in 2018. And it's a trend that you're likely to feel as well, whether you read this in 2018 or even 2027.

What's the trend? It's those darn Millennials, those in America's population who were born between the 1980s and early 2000s. "Gen Y," as the media likes to call them.

When it comes to real estate, Millennials tend to rent. Millennials are renting for longer than their parents did and are choosing to start a family later in life, putting their career first and focusing on experiences rather than buying assets. This tendency places them in sharp contrast to those retiring today, America's "Baby Boomer" generation. Unlike the Baby Boomers, Millennials don't want to own property. This creates a problem for the Boomers who are now looking to sell off their assets and retire on the returns.

Naturally, there are still plenty of Baby Boomers able to sell property. These sales are typically not to Millennials. And, as Millennials become the largest group of potential buyers, the generation's interest in renting seems a cause for concern, adding to reduced home ownership rates across the US.

A concern to the Baby Boomers, at least. To you the investor, however, the trend away from home ownership (with the Boomers) and towards renting (with the Millennials) is very encouraging. You can delight in the fact that home ownership levels are declining to as low as 60%. For every 1% decline, that means an additional 1 million units of housing that will be needed for the non-buyers (aka renters), and this means opportunity for us as investors.

Equally encouraging is the fact that Millennials rent to live close to where they work, drink, and otherwise interact/socialize with friends. This is great news for you because it means Millennials will be more interested in your rental properties.

Finally, it's good to know that Millennials have a practical, economic basis for renting. In other words, their desire to rent and be "near the action" isn't just a passing, youthful phase. With the amount of crippling student debt that most members of "Gen Y" are saddled with, along with rising house prices and stagnant wage growth, Millennials lack the kind of financial stability required to break into the housing market. Their incomes tend to be low and stay that way as wages in the US remain about the same overall.

The bottom line then is that, by and large, the US is trending to more of a renting nation, and this represents a significant—and positive—trend in multifamily. Take comfort in this trend and be sure to consider its implications in your efforts.

#5 - Growing Rental Trends

On the heels of #4 comes another closely related factor, growing rental trends, which is a formal way of saying that rents are increasing.

Whenever you see increases, you can infer that the local economy is healthy and stable. Increasing rents indicate a "good" local economy since people in an area can afford to pay more to live in the area. You'll therefore have less risk as an investor since you can raise rents and find tenants at the new levels.

#6 - Affordable Housing Market and Neighborhoods

For this sixth factor in determining the "right" area to invest, you'll be looking at the rent against value (RV) ratio on potential investments in the area.

The RV ratio, a percent, is determined by dividing the monthly gross rent by the acquisition price. As percentages go, anything less than 1% won't work for you. The reason is that 1% indicates a property or area will be too expensive for you to achieve cash flow. RV ratios also work in the opposite direction. If you see one that's over 1.5%, that should give you equal pause. Anything higher than 1.5% indicates the area could be a depressed market or a neighborhood in economic decline.

An example would be Detroit. In mentioning this city, let me be clear: I have nothing personally against Detroit. Nonetheless, the city does make an easy "punching bag" in discussions of where caution is advised. It's hard to get excited considering how much Detroit has suffered, especially since 2008. From losing a huge employer (General Motors) to having much of its population leave to filing for bankruptcy (as a city), Detroit hasn't exactly been on the "up and up." So it seems fair to describe Detroit as a prime case of a "depressed market." But the optimist in me also thinks that what goes down must come up.

Be careful with Detroit and similar cases, when the RV ratio is above 1.5%. The numbers are essentially warning you that "if it seems too good to be true, it probably is." Heed their advice and look instead for areas where the RV ratio is 1.2-1.4%.

» Rule of Thumb: When calculating RV ratios, the ideal range is 1.2-1.4%.

#7 - Landlord-Friendly Laws

Landlord-friendly laws make an additional, albeit "softer," factor to assess regarding markets for REI. I say "softer" because this factor is somewhat open to interpretation. After all, my sense of "friendly" may be what you'd deem "unfriendly." Overall, though, this term refers to US states where the laws favor the landlord. These states are usually ones where the population tends to vote overwhelmingly for America's Republican party in political elections. For that reason, we'd term such states as "red." Texas and North Carolina are examples of red states.

The opposite are "blue" states, where the population tends to support America's other political party—the Democrats. In "blue" states, the laws are typically less landlord-friendly and more tenant-friendly.

The importance of laws in either direction is that they indicate how easy or difficult it will be for you to manage your property. At the same time, don't view landlord-friendly laws as a "make or break" thing. New York, for example, is a "blue" state and I had plenty of success there with my early investments. So laws for landlords are more a "nice to have," icing-on-the-proverbial-cake kind of thing.

#8 - Thriving or Emerging Downtown

A final litmus test in judging where to invest will be the existence of a thriving or emerging downtown. Like test #7 (above), this one is also a "nice to have." The downtown area(s) here can typically be found in many "tier 2" cities across the US. Since 2008, such cities have seen a resurgence in their downtown section(s). The resurgence is due to changing renter habits, as Millennials, among others, rent longer and want proximity to work and to nightlife. The result is a flourishing, often unexpectedly, in the downtown and formerly depressed regions of certain cities. Cases where we see this happening include Cincinnati, OH, Pittsburgh, PA, and Memphis, TN.

PROPERTY CLASSES AND MARKET CLASSES

Property classes and market classes aren't a litmus test. They're still fundamentally important when considering where to invest. Plus, since we mentioned "Class B" properties earlier, it only fits that we explain the other types too.

Let's begin with property classes. We'll define them as "A," "B," and "C." Properties that are considered "Class A" are those that have been built in the last fifteen years. "Class B" properties, in turn, are those built in the 1980s to 1990s. After this type are "Class C" properties, which were built in the 1960s to 1980s. Anything older than the 1950s could then potentially be considered "Class D." I say "potentially" because Class D properties are often historical ones, where the historical status puts the properties in a different league than other places that are simply old.

Property classes are vital to you the investor since they indicate the amount of work you'll be required to do on a property. Class A properties, for example, will likely have little in the way of deferred maintenance that needs to be done. The recent construction of such properties explains that. Class C and Class D properties, though, could need substantial maintenance. I found this out for myself with some of my upstate New York properties. One issue I found to be problematic in older houses were cast iron pipes. Cast iron pipes are a relatively old way to plumb a house and hence fixing them ended up requiring a tremendous amount of money. Given that such work costs money, I strongly advise you to be aware of property classes before investing. That way you'll have a clear sense of how much investment will be required should you purchase a particular property.

In addition to property classes, make sure you understand market classes. We define market classes around the desirability and the types of people in an area. Class A markets are those with nearly universal appeal. In my market, Los Angeles, examples of Class A markets are Beverly Hills and Santa Monica. Most people who live or want to live in LA would be happy to reside in those two "Class A" markets. Think of Class A as where demand outstrips supply for renters.

After "Class A" markets, you'll also see "Class B" markets. These markets are cheaper to live in than "A" and tend to have young professionals. Personally, I'm a big fan of "Class B" markets since the tenants tend to be gainfully employed. In the right Class B submarkets, these areas tend to be in the Path of Progress

I'm not opposed, though, to "Class C" markets. "C" denotes a market with more of a "blue collar," working-class vibe. Residents of these areas are typically there as a result of economic circumstances, such as losing their job.

Class D and below denotes high-crime, low- income areas, similar to the Baltimore neighborhood I described in earlier chapters.

• • • • • • • • •

That does it on classes and litmus tests. Armed with everything we've covered here in Step 2, you'll be better equipped to identify potential markets for RE investing. You can now use the preceding material to create a "shortlist" of possible markets.

Don't do that yet, however. Keep reading so you can learn two more essential steps in the process of choosing the "right" market. The next two steps allow you to confidently move from having a "shortlist" of potential markets to selecting one particular market.

STEP 3: MARKET ANALYSIS

For the third step, select two markets from your "shortlist." Once you've chosen the two markets, go online to a website such as Craigslist.com, loopnet.com or Showcase.com. Look around the site at the properties that are currently up for sale and rent. Then select as many of these properties as you can and begin crunching the numbers. Your goal is to see how these supposed "deals" stack up alongside one another.

Analyzing actual deals in a market will indicate what cash flow opportunities—if any—exist for you there. Depending on the particular market, you may find, for example, that such opportunities are few and far between. Or crunching the numbers may reveal just the opposite. You may see that a market has even more REI potential than you imagined.

To crunch the numbers on the deals you find, I recommend using a spreadsheet. As a benefit to you, I've shared my spreadsheet tool online. Go to www.dealanalytica.com and type in the code ***CRACKIN*** to get a FREE 30-day access to my online underwriting service.

With my spreadsheet or your own, take the time now to analyze at least twenty-five deals per market. This means if you're looking at two markets, you'll be analyzing a minimum of fifty different deals.

Twenty-five deals per market means twenty-five deals per market. Not ten deals for a market you prefer and forty deals for the one you're in doubt on. No, twenty-five deals *per market*.

It'll take you some time, that's for sure. And it isn't sexy. The benefit, though, is that analyzing at least twenty-five deals in a market will help you get a feel for typical market metrics and trends. These metrics/trends will only become apparent to you through analyzing deals in a market by the truckload. Among everything you'll be seeing, here are a few of particular note:

- Average cost/door of comparable deals (In multifamily investing, this is referred to as the "price/door.")
- Rent per unit
- Rent per square foot (Apartment rent divided by apartment size in square feet)
- Typical vacancy and occupancy rates
- Cap rates: In-place NOI / Asking Price
- Expense ratios (Total expenses divided by income)
- Trends in a surrounding suburb
- Average rent per suburb
- Taxes
- Average utility cost

Analyzing deals, like much of REI, can seem overwhelming to you at first. Let me be a broken record here and reiterate my ongoing emphasis on staying calm. You *can* do this. Don't write yourself off just because there are a ton of terms and some analysis. Trust me when I say you'll be an expert in no time. It's not rocket science.

If it helps, know that I was in your shoes at one point. I remember feeling very overwhelmed, for example, when trying to analyze my early properties. It was terrifying for me to think of missing crucial details and making a bad investment. Especially in the early years, when I had access to far less savings and investment capital than today. What inspired me then, and can inspire you now, is two things.

First, there's the familiar refrain "If Reed can do it, so can you." And it's true!

After that, your other source of inspiration can be the "Law of large numbers." This is the idea that large numbers don't lie. If you analyze twenty-five or even fifty deals in a market and see nothing but "crackers," well, you might want to be quiet about it. It could be a mistake to go blabbing about the gold mine of deals you have found. The reason is that you may have stumbled on a great market. (Feel free to tell me all about it, though!)

Large numbers protect you against a few isolated exceptions. And this offers definite reassurance to you, as an investor, when vetting potential markets.

Also, to aid you in your search for information online, I'll be providing a host of great websites at the end of this chapter. One that I'm particularly fond of is www.reis.com. It's a site which belongs to the leading market reporting agency (REIS).

Using Reis.com will seemingly "set you back" a few hundred dollars, or more, due to the cost. I'd argue that it will actually "set you forward" in terms of the credible market data the site provides. With REIS, you'll get reliable information on rents, vacancies, loss to lease, and most importantly, cap rates. Having this vital information and being able to depend on it will make all the difference in your investment decisions. For that reason, we can probably both agree that a few hundred is a small price compared to the thousands or more you'd potentially be earning from investments in a market. If you aren't keen on spending money on market data papers from REIS.com, there are plenty of other ways you can achieve the same thing for free, but it will take a bit of your time. Head over to reedgoossens.com/books to get a list to help you complete a comprehensive review of a particular US market.

STEP 4: VISIT THE AREA – BEFORE YOU INVEST!

This last step is the "moment of truth." It's what guarantees you don't end up with a $15K drug-den house.

Hopefully, your visit doesn't include syringes. Even if it doesn't, though, you may still be turned off from a market. Perhaps you'll find something that's less immediate yet still troubling.

Whatever it is, you won't know until you visit the area. Visiting is the only way for you—especially if you're a foreign investor—to understand where you're potentially buying. One or more meaningful visits allow you to get your bearings and establish credibility, and allows you to "touch and feel" the local market and discover growth corridors. It also enables you to begin building your "A-team."

Your "A-Team" for REI will be made up of those professionals who can provide top quality, "boots on the ground" support to you and your investment. You'll be able to depend on them, even if you're not in the market where you've invested.

Who are these people? And how do you find them?

That's the subject of our next chapter. Join me on the following pages for all the details on developing your A-Team.

WEBSITES FOR RESEARCH

- REIS (Reis.com)
- Economic Development Directory (Ecodevdirectory.com) – A great resource for finding indicators on economic developments around the US and worldwide too.

- The US Bureau of Labor Statistics (Bls.gov) – Solid employment data directly from the US government.

- Marcus & Millichap (Marcusmillichap.com) – A leader in apartment market research.

- REI Club (reiclub.com/real-estate-articles.php) – Home to many quality articles on REI.

- The US Census Bureau (Census.gov) – Offering population data and showing MSAs.

- Multifamily Executive (Multifamilyexecutive.com) – The place to find news on the multifamily industry.

- Multifamily Housing News (Multihousingnews.com) – Another trusty spot for news on the multifamily industry.

- Renting (Rentpingmedia.com) – A site for in-house apartment marketing.

- Affordable Housing Finance (Housingfinance.com) – A website on housing and multifamily news with a distinctly financial angle.

- CoStar (Costar.com) – A leading commercial real estate information site.

- Google (Google.com) – What? I mean it! Google is a great tool for determining market unemployment and population trends.

COMFORT CHALLENGE

Time for a comfort challenge. For this one, I want you to take action on choosing a market. I've given you all the steps in this chapter. It's time now to get off the proverbial bench and figure out where you're going to invest.

As you follow the steps, your process will include choosing five markets that you think you understand. Then, you'll be listing out the population, jobs, GDP growth, and other stats for this market. Put all the stats on an Excel sheet.

Framing the details side-by-side in Excel will show you how the markets stack up and whether your assumptions are truly "on the money." From there, head over to LoopNet.com if you're thinking of large commercial properties. Or, if you'd prefer residential properties (four units and under), get on Trulia.com and start researching.

Also, in giving you this comfort challenge, I hope to further emphasize some of the most important parts of the market selection phase. Nothing in this challenge is meant to replace the steps. Make sure you do everything I've described earlier. I'm simply highlighting a few particular parts of the process with this comfort challenge.

Make sense? Good, now go and find your ideal REI market.

★★ AUSSIE-ISMS ★★

We'll go a bit lighter on the Aussie-isms for this chapter. That way it won't distract you from the flood of data you'll encounter when doing market research and analyzing deals.

1. "Have a Crack" – To give something a try; What you'll be doing with deal analysis after reading this chapter (hint, hint!)

2. Macca's – McDonalds; Where you'll have to eat all your meals if you don't properly analyze a deal.

3. Devo – Devastated; The state of your body if you eat at Macca's too much.

4. Acting like a flaming gala! – Acting crazy.

5. "Rubber necking" – Tourists admiring/staring at something of interest.

CHAPTER 6

DEVELOPING YOUR A-TEAM: BOOTS ON THE GROUND (MINI CHAPTER)

There's no "I" in Team.

Ever heard that one?

Chances are you have. It's a cliché, used everywhere from sports to corporate management.

I mention it now because we're going to talk about teams in an area where the "I" matters.

REI.

Try spelling *that* without the letter "I."

Naturally, you can't. Yet with REI, the "I" doesn't stand for "individual" Instead, it stands for investment.

Investment, in the real estate sense, is hardly a solo pursuit. It requires collaboration with others to successfully make deals and achieve favorable returns.

How exactly do you "collaborate?"

Perhaps the most obvious way to collaborate is with sellers directly, engaging with them to buy their properties.

Another instance of collaboration, one that's far greater in scope, involves collaborating with those on an investing team you've assembled.

This chapter focuses on the second case, providing tips to help you develop your investing team.

Why have an investing team?

One reason is that you can't do everything yourself. Especially if you're working a 9-to-5 job right now and planning to do REI part time.

Even if you're committed full time to REI, you still can't properly do everything yourself. You'll need the assistance of experts.

The ideal way to obtain help as a real estate investor is to have a team of people you can rely on for your various needs. You use smartphone apps, right? But doesn't mean you're incapable. It simply means you sometimes need direction. Google Maps, anyone?

People aren't apps, but your team members will *app*-ly their knowledge and skills to help you.

One of the best ways you'll get help is finding "crackin'" deals.

And not just finding them, but sealing them *first*, before anyone else knows about the deals.

This is the key to building a portfolio that yields incredible returns: finding the crackin' rental properties before they become public knowledge. When these "best-kept secrets" are truly "best-kept secrets," they're the holy grail. Real estate investing is the only business where insider secrets are completely legal.

If you want to be successful in REI, then you've got to have a team, which you create through networking and establishing good relationships with professionals like CPAs, lawyers, and real estate agents. As your portfolio grows and you continue to prove yourself as a successful real estate investor, you'll attract more team members into your orbit, which will snowball into further success for you.

The team you create should consist of seven people, each of whom engage in a line of work that enables them to aid your REI efforts.

Who are these seven people?

TEAM MEMBER #1 - REAL ESTATE BROKER

Real estate brokers traditionally work with sellers and buyers in real estate transactions. They serve as the listing agents for a seller's property, for example, or they help buyers find suitable properties.

Real estate brokers must be constantly attuned to the market and have their fingers on the "pulse" of what's going on with potential buyers and sellers. This quality makes real estate brokers extremely valuable to you. By having one on your team, you can get insights on crackin' deals, just as they're emerging. A good real estate broker will send you leads on such deals and enable you to swoop in as the proverbial "early bird."

Establishing credibility with brokers as a neophyte investor can be tough, but it's of paramount importance to your success in that particular market. You will need to increase your marketing efforts tenfold so that brokers will think of you and give you a chance. Whether it's through meeting for a meal, going out for drinks, or playing a few rounds of golf (full disclosure: I am a complete hack, but fortunately, my business partner is a golfing guru), you need to be willing to go the extra mile to get noticed in your chosen market.

You will also need to be consistent in your follow-up with brokers. Always provide feedback on deals they send your way even if they aren't a fit for your investing criteria. The more effort you put in to broker relationships, the more it will pay off in the long run. I spend a lot of energy building quality relationships with brokers in my chosen markets.

Tips for establishing solid relationships with brokers:

1. Be willing to meet face-to-face with brokers for a meal or drinks. Your aim should be to meet all the major brokers in your market.

2. Build out your investment pitch deck to include information about your background, your past deals (if any), and your investment criteria. Providing a broker with a professional-looking document goes a long way towards establishing your credibility. If you want to know more about how to develop your pitch deck, check out my website at www.reedgoossens.com.

3. Be consistent with your follow-up; solid broker relationships take time to develop, like any good relationship. Always respond to brokers who send you deals, even if they aren't a fit for your business. Highlight why a particular deal might not fit your investing needs so they can better target their proposals next time. The best way to build credibility is to be a closer. The more deals you close, the more investment opportunities will come your way.

A broker will help you find crackin' deals!

TEAM MEMBER #2 - PROPERTY INSPECTOR

A property inspector will inspect the property you're considering. In doing so, they'll be looking for both existing problems and areas that could prove problematic later.

Among the things they'll examine:

- Electricity
- Plumbing
- Heating
- Air conditioning
- Vents
- Water
- Foundation issues
- General upkeep of the asset, including the inside and outside structure
- Roofing issues
- Structural issues and defects
- Potential code violations
- Much more

Depending on what the property inspector finds, you have a few options. You can require that the seller complete the repairs prior to closing, renegotiate with the seller on the purchase price, or simply walk away from the deal if the issues with the property are too cumbersome to assume. A good property inspector will save you a lot of money. The fee you pay the inspector is bound to be well below the price you'd pay for buying a lemon and likely a lot less than the cost of repairs. How much less? It depends on the size of the property.

For a large property, one with hundreds of units, you're probably looking at $3,000–$4,000 for an inspector. For a small property, you'll likely pay $300–$400. For example, I recently paid an inspector $3,750 to inspect a 192-unit asset I purchased in San Antonio, TX.

Make sure you don't hire just any property inspector. Find one with experience and expertise in building and safety, HVAC, and structural issues. You can do that by consulting with a real estate agent or asking other local investors whom they recommend. Agents are already in the real estate business, so they're bound to know at least a few good property inspectors.

Once you have an inspector, ensure their inspection includes a thorough check of both the inside and outside of your desired property. It's also important for you to communicate clearly with the property inspector so they know what you want the inspection to cover. Be sure you know what you're looking for, too.

Provided that you and the inspector are on the same page, they can provide a useful and reliable assessment of whether a property is worth purchasing. This assessment is usually worth its weight in gold, since property inspectors operate as independent third parties.

Before you sign on the dotted line to purchase a property, review everything the inspector has found. This relates back to what we said about avoiding deals you don't understand. If you receive a property inspection report and are unclear about its findings, ask for an explanation and don't settle until you fundamentally understand all of the issues with the property, so you can make an informed decision about next steps.

TEAM MEMBER #3 - PROPERTY MANAGER

The third essential member of your team should be a property manager. The property manager (PM) will serve as your "boots on the ground" team member. They'll be on-site to oversee the day-to-day operations of a particular property in your investment portfolio.

Of the team members we've covered so far, a PM is undoubtedly the most important one because he or she has the most control over your investments and the resulting cash flows you'll receive.

An inept PM can cause your property to have a high vacancy rate or bad tenants, both of which will lead to lost revenue and, with it, lower investment returns.

Given the potential damage a bad PM can do, it's imperative that you find one who has experience managing the type of asset you are buying. In addition, you'll want a capable or even exceptional PM on your team from an efficiency standpoint. Remember, the goal is to make your real estate investments run like clockwork, so everything hums along smoothly at your properties while you sit back and collect income.

If you aspire to reach that point, you will need a PM who's skilled enough to take over and effectively handle all aspects of your property. This way, you're freed from having to personally manage day-to-day operations.

How do you tell whether a PM is actually capable and up to the task?

Here are some questions you can ask those you interview for a spot on your REI team.

Note: While these questions are focused more on PMs who manage 50+ units, these principles can also be applied to PMs at multifamily properties of all sizes and to single-family homes.

Questions to Ask When Assessing a Property Manager

Question 1 - What size properties are they currently managing?

You don't want to end up with a PM who only has experience managing single-family homes if you're looking for someone to manage your 100-unit property, or vice versa.

Question 2 - What do the PM's current and past clients say about them?

Obtaining client references from PM candidates is important because they accomplish two things for you.

First, they'll give you a sense of the PM's past and current performance.

Make sure you *actually* contact the references. Every last one of them. Pick up the phone and just do it. Otherwise, as with any REI reference-checking, you'll be taking an unnecessary and utterly preventable risk.

When you contact the references ask them questions like:

- How responsive is the PM?
- Are they transparent and forthcoming in sharing quotes from general contractors who complete work on the reference's property?
- How do they deal with evictions and what's their eviction process?
- Do they encourage tenant retention?

By asking these kinds of questions of the reference, you'll be able to measure the PM's capabilities.

If the reference doesn't have an answer for any of the questions above, you should ask the PM directly or request another reference. Having all of the questions answered is imperative so you can eliminate the risk of hiring a bad PM.

The less obvious, second benefit of references is networking. Whether or not you actually hire a given PM, the references they provide to you are new contacts who invest in your market. You should add these people to your rolodex and seek to network with them. Who knows? They might someday join your REI team or become potential future investors in your deals.

Question 3 - What's the PM's experience with repositioning multifamily properties?

Note: this question tends to be more suited to multifamily PMs

If a PM has repositioned other properties in the area, you'll want to know which ones so you can go and "walk them." Ask them to tell you about their experience(s).

Walking the properties gives you a sense of two things:

1. The PM's ability to handle a repositioning.

2. The properties' finishes and amenities, which are good to know since the repositioned properties may be your competition. Even if they're not your competition, they'll simply serve as a comparable for your renovation budget and analysis.

Question 4 - Does the PM have a general contractor on staff? Or do they outsource to third-party subcontractors?

General contractors (GCs) and subcontractors handle the physical work that a property requires. Your PM will rely on them to handle issues like A/C and plumbing repairs, roofing, electrical problems, etc. Therefore, it's important to know how a particular PM works with GCs and subcontractors.

Do they, for example, have a GC on staff? If so, does this GC have a license and insurance? Or does the PM employ a jack-of-all-trades handyman?

> Note: the larger the property management company, the more likely it is that they'll have a GC on staff (this applies for PMs who manage both single-family homes and multifamily portfolios).

If the PM uses subcontractors, you'll need to ask about their vetting and hiring process. Do they obtain three quotes for each major trades-person who's being considered (e.g., HVAC, roofing, electrical, etc.)? Or does the PM simply skip the quotes and hire a jack-of-all-trades to complete the work?

Also, does the PM have preferred subcontractors they tend to use on all of their projects?

Ask the PM about scheduling, which is important when considering work that a subcontractor will need to complete. You'll need to ask whether a PM imposes a schedule and if they require subcontractors to sign contracts stipulating the schedule and other work details.

I realize that these contractor-related questions are a lot for you to consider. Despite the volume of questions, don't be overwhelmed or skip anything outlined here. This batch of contractor-related questions is just as important as the others because they're meant to give you comfort on the type, quality, and pricing of the work you'll get from your PMs, GCs, and subcontractors.

Furthermore, these contractor questions reveal whether the PM can ably advise you. You'll come to see whether they're knowledgeable about the right type of unit rehab for your property and how best to spend your capital expenditure (CAPEX) dollars to maximize rents and your returns. Does the PM know what unit rehab is needed in order to achieve premium rents for the submarket? Ask the right questions and you'll know for sure.

Question 5 - What's the PM's knowledge of material specifications?

Any PM that you seriously consider should be able to advise you on material specifications. These relate to the types of finishes that will achieve premium rents and the associated cost or cost per square foot for individual items (e.g., countertops, flooring, painting, siding).

To determine whether a PM is proficient in this area, ask them for specifications ("specs"). This is a list of everything that's required to maximize rents and be competitive in your submarket. The list includes such things as the types of finishes, flooring, light fixtures, and countertops that will yield the best returns.

> Note: Make sure to document the various specs you use for different finishes and keep track of them as you complete more deals. Over time, you'll develop your own "spec book" and you'll gain a better sense of exact costs. This will help you better estimate the financial outlay.

Possessing this knowledge will be tremendously useful to you when walking potential properties. As you review them, you'll find areas for possible renovation. With a knowledge of the specs, you'll have a good sense of what it typically costs to complete those renovations. This intuitive sense will then help you develop a more accurate construction budget.

Question 6 - How does the PM fare when checking the assumptions in your analysis?

A good PM will have no difficulty reviewing your analysis and letting you know if any of your assumptions are wrong and need to be changed, particularly when it comes to the assumptions you might have made relating to the operating budget for a particular property.

Personally, I always send them my spreadsheet analysis of the potential deal. When I do this, I'm specifically looking to get the prospective PM's feedback on items like:

- Rent increases for the area
- The expense ratio
- Utility charges
- Bill-back systems
- Additional income expenses
- Whether tenants will pay the fees on those additional income expenses (e.g., carport rents, storage rents, vending machine costs, etc.)
- Operating (OPEX) budgets

I suggest you get in the habit of requesting feedback on any underwriting from a seasoned PM. It's a real litmus test in my opinion. If the PM can provide great feedback and quality advice, they deserve a lot of "brownie points."

Question 7 - What's the PM's tenant screening process?

Tenants are the lifeblood of your investment property. Thus, you'll need to ask the PM how they go about screening tenants.

At a minimum, you'll want to hear that a prospective PM undertakes the following:

- Completes background checks
- Runs a credit history and employment verification check
- Only accepts tenants with an employment history (with the same employer) of at least six months [Note: Every situation is different; however, a six-month minimum employment term is a good starting point]
- Checks a potential tenant's rental references from past landlords

Question 8 - What applications and rental agreements does the PM use with potential tenants?

For this question, you're asking the PM for a copy of their rental agreement with tenants. If you're new to the REI game, make sure to review these agreements with a lawyer or someone who knows what to look for.

From my own experience, I'd advise you to consider the following key items in applications and agreements, which will vary from state to state):

- Eviction and default clauses for when tenants fail to comply with any of the financial or material provisions of the agreement
- Deposit requirements
- Subleasing clauses should indicate no subleasing allowed
- Tenant liability clauses should state something to the effect of,

"Each tenant(s) is jointly and individually liable for all Lease Agreement obligations..."

- Renewal clauses and notices

- Use of premises clause, which is a clause that includes language like, "The Premises shall be used and occupied by Tenant(s), for no more than FOUR (4) persons exclusively, as a private individual dwelling, and no part of the Premises shall be used sub-leasing at any time during the term of this Agreement."

- Move-out clauses, or a "Surrender of premises" clause, which requires the tenant to leave the unit. Sample language reads, "Tenant(s) shall surrender the Premises in better or equal condition as it was at the commencement of this Agreement, reasonable use, wear and tear thereof, and damages by the elements excepted."

Question 9 - What kind of property management technology does the PM use?

This question will shed light on the different technologies a PM uses or is implementing. Such technologies are used by a PM to make it more convenient for their tenants to pay rent and submit maintenance requests.

Some PMs may argue that not all tenants are online. While this may be true, I still like to see a PM making an effort to get tenants to pay online or to provide a system that makes payment easier (for example, a computer in the leasing office that tenants can use to pay their rent online).

Follow my lead on this. Look for PMs who are always learning and implementing new systems to make rent collection, evictions, and late notices as smooth and easy as possible.

TEAM MEMBER #4 - GENERAL CONTRACTOR

Coming in fourth on your team, though no less important than any others, is the general contractor (GC).

In addition to everything we've covered earlier, it's important to understand that we're now talking about your own knowledge of GCs rather than a prospective PM's knowledge of GCs. You'll want to be knowledgeable about GCs, subcontractors, and others who can perform maintenance-related work at your property.

I recommend lining up a local team of GCs who can fix issues at your property on a moment's notice. As you might expect, this will give you tremendous peace of mind, especially if you're investing from out of state or from overseas.

A local GC (or ideally a team of GCs) is also a great source of information on pricing for large repair jobs. They should be knowledgeable about the proper local costs of repair items like roofs, siding, HVAC, plumbing, and more. All of the aforementioned items are among those that you, as an investor, may need to fix at your property. With the right locally-based GCs, you won't be taken to the cleaners on pricing for such repairs.

The GC should also be knowledgeable about local building codes, be able to identify if a property has building violations, and have a good working relationship with the local municipality's building and safety department. The answers to these questions will also help you educate yourself on the process by which GCs need to obtain work permits if they are doing large renovations to your property.

TEAM MEMBER #5 - REAL ESTATE ATTORNEY

Lawyers...

Slimy, no-good, and spineless?

Or righteous, helpful, and principled?

Whatever your opinion, you can't realistically succeed at long-term REI without a capable real estate attorney. The right attorney will be based locally in the market where you're investing because the legal requirements associated with investing in a given market vary from jurisdiction to jurisdiction, particularly in the US, and lawyers in the US are licensed to practice at the state level. A lawyer from New York might not be knowledgeable about the local laws of Florida nor admitted to practice in the Sunshine State. Your RE attorney can help you buy and invest correctly from a legal standpoint. You won't run the risk, for example, of accidentally violating some rarely cited, but very costly, legal statute. A qualified RE attorney will help you avoid such pitfalls.

Let's now consider the attributes you should consider in hiring a locally-based RE lawyer.

Experience

Does the real estate attorney you're considering know their stuff? If they're seasoned, you'll be in for a smooth real estate transaction. Has the lawyer been practicing in the local real estate market for many years or are they a relative newcomer to the jurisdiction or the practice of law?

In the latter case, you might want to avoid working with such an attorney. Nothing personal, of course. It's only that a criminal justice lawyer, for example, who's now trying their hand at real estate settlements probably isn't your best choice. You're better off considering the attorneys with the most real estate experience.

Comfort with Technology

Your real estate attorney doesn't need to be the legal world's equivalent of Mark Zuckerberg. If you want an attorney who's been analyzing real estate laws since the age of eight, knock yourself out. But that's not necessary. However, at the very least you'll need an attorney who's comfortable using email and digital signatures and performing remote closings. I live in Los Angeles, but I close on deals all the time in Texas. I have never physically attended a closing of one of my properties.

Local Knowledge

Knowledge may be power, but it's not enough in matters of real estate law. Your real estate attorney can't just be knowledgeable about general real estate laws. They must also fully understand the local process for real estate transactions and stay abreast of the latest events and changes to the laws that could impact the process. All of that local knowledge and awareness will enable a real estate attorney to properly represent you.

Speaking of representation, it's worth noting that, barring any unforeseen problems, a real estate attorney's role is usually relatively minor until the end of the transaction.

Their role includes representing you and helping you complete the lender's paperwork, negotiating the purchase and sales agreement with the seller, and reviewing the title policy. An RE attorney will also help you anticipate problems before they occur and handle such problems for you if they arise. Hiccups during a transaction, like issues with title and or pre-existing liens, can be quite stressful.

However, a skilled real estate attorney will make the transaction as stress-free as possible.

TEAM MEMBER #6 - TITLE COMPANY

In the United States, a title company is usually a third-party company that makes sure the title to a piece of real estate is clean. They search for any liens on the property and will then issue title insurance for that property. Title insurance protects the lender and owner against lawsuits or claims against the property that result from disputes over the title, which might stem from issues that arose prior to your ownership.

Investors new to the US will be surprised to learn that title companies are typically third-party companies. In contrast, in Australia, title issues are typically dealt with by the attorney rather than by a third party. Furthermore, title insurance, which protects the buyer from claims arising from prior ownership of the property, might be a concept new to international investors. I was surprised to hear such insurance existed when I first moved to the US, but here in a country known for its litigiousness, everyone is looking to protect themselves, hence the necessity for title insurance.

Dealing with title companies and title insurance in the US may seem like a burden, and it adds costs at the closing table, but the title company is a necessary member of your team.

Word of advice: Like your real estate attorney, your title company should possess local knowledge of the market in which you are investing. I recently experienced a major issue with one of my transactions when the seller insisted on using an out-of-state title company. Needless to say, last-minute issues arose relating to a common easement on the property, which had the potential to derail the entire deal. If we had had a local title company, they would have known how to deal with

> *this easement issue promptly and would have helped us avoid the last-minute stress that ensued in trying to resolve the problem.*

TEAM MEMBER #7 - CPA (TAX ADVISOR)

A certified public accountant (CPA) or tax advisor is one of those indispensable people who belongs on any REI team. When you own real estate in the US, a qualified and seasoned CPA is essential so that you know your tax liability. You need to know what you owe on your properties versus how much depreciation or how many expenses you can write off.

If you're still unclear on the basics of depreciation and other tax-related items, I'd encourage you to reread our earlier chapter on taxes so that you're clear on how they work.

Reading alone won't suffice, however, when it comes to taxes. You will still need a CPA on your team. To find one, and many of the other people on your team, I recommend turning to either real estate forums or a Yelp search. Either can help in your initial search. I also recommend using NRTA for those international investors looking for a great tax advisor who deals solely with foreign owners.

Once you've found a candidate who seems viable, as with any other team member, be sure to obtain references. It's the only way to really know that you're working with reputable people who have your best interests at heart.

• • • • • • • • •

With all this talk about teams, let's not forget about the most important person of all.

You!

You need a strong and qualified team, no question.

Yet even with a team, you still need to educate yourself and be aware of how real estate investment works in the US.

Your teammates *can help* you. We're not saying they *will* necessarily help you, since you've got to know what you need help on. You're your own best advocate.

And we're also not suggesting that those on your team do your thinking for you. At least not when it comes to the personal and meaningful decisions you'll need to make. You should seek and receive guidance and advice on those things from your team, of course. But such decisions are ultimately yours alone to make.

To make the right decisions, you'll need, in addition to a team, a solid education. Which is where this book comes in. So, keep reading, and we'll make sure that the most important person on your team is a top performer!

★ ★ REED-ISMS ★ ★

My number one saying is:

"A fool and their money are easily parted" – Lee Goossens

Crackin' Deals: A Smoking hot deal!

CHAPTER 7

REVIEWING THE HERD

"Review the herd."

It's an Aussie phrase, originating with the farmers who'd review their herds of cattle. Since those days, the term has evolved to mean taking stock of a situation. Seeing where you're at, personally or in relation to others.

Reviewing the herd isn't just for Aussies and ranchers. We're going to be doing it too. That's the focus of this chapter. It only fits, too, since we're about halfway through this book.

In this chapter, I'll help you to "review the herd" on a personal level. This means that we'll be looking at where you are with regard to REI. To do that, we'll be going over a set of seven key questions. How you answer each of these questions will then give you a sense of your willingness and capability to truly enter REI.

Let's begin now with those seven key questions.

KEY QUESTION #1 – DO YOU WANT TO BE A FULL-TIME OR A PART-TIME RE INVESTOR?

This question comes first since it gives you a frame for assessing how involved you want to be in REI.

My recommendation is to look at your financial situation. Chances are you probably don't have the money up front to abruptly quit your full-time job and go straight into REI. If that's your situation, you can take confidence in the fact that you're following in the footsteps of many REI legends.

A prime example would be Arnold Schwarzenegger. He had a job paying $300 per week and about $12,000 saved from an early film, *Hercules in New York*. These sources allowed him to go part time into REI without drowning financially. You may not have abs like Arnold, but like the "Austrian Oak," you do have a full-time job to aid in your initial, part-time REI efforts.

Another example for part-time REI would be me. In my case, I began in REI while working full time at my engineering job in NYC. Eventually, I quit that job and moved out to the Los Angeles area. Even then I still didn't go fully into REI. Instead, I stayed a part-time real estate investor and worked full time on my consulting business.

This raises the question then of what exactly constitutes "full-time" versus "part-time" REI. For full time, I'd classify it as having all or at least the majority of your income coming from REI. If you're in this position, you're probably also working full time, either to manage your investments or to further build your portfolio. Your situation here differs from those in REI "part time." We can define part time as working a "9 to 5" and then having real estate be your "5 to 9," an after-work *side hustle*.

With all the emphasis on doing REI part time, I realize you may feel confused. Wasn't the first chapter of this book all about how I took a huge leap and made a move to the US? And haven't I also bashed the "9 to 5," leaving it as bruised as the fighters in *Rocky*? Yes and yes. There's no contradiction, though, because I've also emphasized the need to be pragmatic and realistic.

That's why, for example, we're asking these important questions now. I want you to think before you get swept up in the REI fervor. Part of the questioning process means realizing that you don't know how long it will take to obtain your first real estate property. Will it be a month? Several months? A year? I can't say, and chances are you can't either. And that's just property number one. Who knows how long it will take you to obtain enough investment properties that the total income from your portfolio replaces that of your current job?

Concerns like these reinforce my case for part-time REI, at least initially. So, too, does the amount of time and research required when looking for suitable investment properties. You'll have to find the right property and then conduct due diligence to make sure everything checks out. The Internet makes this easier, but as my Baltimore story indicated, it's still imperative to see any potential investment in person.

Another reason why I advise part-time REI, in the beginning, is that you don't know how your rental property (or properties) will perform. There are certainly times when you may hit the jackpot with your first rental property. You may, for example, buy a triplex at a great deal and have it fully rented out at market-competitive rates. But perhaps your jackpot proves short-lived. Say a tenant moves out on you soon after. In that case, you've suddenly got a rental property with a third fewer renters, and you've lost rental income from the departed tenant. What now?

It depends on whether you're beginning REI on a full-time or part-time basis. Those who've jumped into REI full time—perhaps against the warnings here—may be thrown into a panic when the tenant leaves.

The part-timers, though, won't feel the same sense of panic. Part-time investors can relax here because there's no economic "gun" to their head. So a tenant moves out. A part-timer now schedules in time, perhaps on their lunch breaks or after work, to focus on finding a new tenant.

Depending on the property's location and their inventiveness, perhaps the part-timer even has some fun with the unit while it's empty. Assuming the property is a few hours away, and in a safe area, maybe the vacancy allows a part-timer to have a mini-vacation there. Talk about turning a negative into a positive. And why not? It's not like the part-time investor is going to be dead-broke now that they've lost some rental income. They still have a full-time job providing ample income to live on and pay the bills. The full-time job also covers any expenses related to the property (mortgages, utility bills, etc.) So why not use the vacant unit as an excuse for a break?

See the difference? It's a night-and-day difference, really, between the reactions of newbie real estate investors in each case. Hopefully, I've made my point on getting started in REI on a part-time versus full-time basis. By now, you can probably tell which one I prefer. You're free, of course, to do as you wish. But if you can't use $100 bills as toilet paper, take my advice—start off part time in REI and let your full-time job support you.

Besides, how do you know that you're even going to like REI? Once you get into the game, suppose you find that it's not for you. Even with some moderate profits from properties. Even with some smooth sailing and perhaps even a big win or two. Maybe you find, on a personal "gut" level, that you'd rather be doing something else. Again, no worries if you're doing this part time. You pick yourself up and move on.

We should probably do that too. Pick up and move on, now that we've covered the first question when thinking about REI.

Following that question, let's examine another.

KEY QUESTION #2 – WHAT FINANCING CAN YOU GET AND HOW MUCH WILL IT BE?

To answer these questions, you'll need to approach financing in a "smart" way. This means avoiding the "dumb" ways of handling your financing, such as blindly guessing or going on incomplete information. Eschew both in favor of accurate knowledge on where you stand financially.

Accurate knowledge entails going through the pre-qualification process for a bank loan. In that process, you'll work with a lender to determine how much money they'd give you if doing a mortgage. Based on what the lender tells you, you'll then be able to look at investment properties within your price range.

Furthermore, relating back to key question #1, as you start out in REI, the income from your full-time job will allow you access to greater leverage from the banks. Banks will determine the size of the loan they are willing to lend based on your salary from your full-time job. Without a full-time job, access to lending is extremely difficult. Another reason to take it slow in the beginning.

In addition, I recommend using an online mortgage calculator to help you visualize the amounts of your monthly payments. This way you'll have accurate knowledge in advance, on both the loan and the payments required to service the loan.

Having accurate knowledge, financially speaking, also means that you're aware of current interest rates and cognizant of which lenders offer the best financing.

With interest rates, make sure to shop around for the lender offering the most competitive rates. Shopping around isn't just a good idea, it's practically a "must." Loans are granted in part on your income ratios, and a measly half a point (0.5%) can push your monthly mortgage payments outside of the acceptable margins to allow a potential investment property to provide cash flow.

Also, as you investigate lenders and their financing packages, don't forget to ask about fees and any other charges that might be tacked on at the end. Asking in advance saves you from any rude awakenings later on. You'll know up front, for example, that the lender expects you to pay for an appraisal, copies of credit reports, a property survey, municipal certificates, and financing fees. These items are, in fact, typically expected by most lenders. So too are "points on your mortgage," financing fees that banks charge you for the pleasure of providing you the service of a great loan that suits your needs. Financing fees can vary from 0.5% to 3% of the loan amount. Depending on the lender, there can be other fees as well. Wondering what those other fees are, exactly? Don't wonder. Ask!

Asking is equally important if you're unable to get a loan based on your credit history. When this occurs, you have the right to ask for a copy of your credit report. Ask and you shall receive it from the "credit gods" (i.e., the reporting agencies). Checking your credit report is imperative here because the agencies do make mistakes. So your credit report may have errors on it that are preventing you from getting a loan. You'll only spot the errors, however, by requesting your report and then reviewing it closely.

A review of your credit history is also a good idea. It fits with my emphasis on knowing yourself and should be a definite step in your assessment before entering the REI world. If you are an international investor, your credit report here in the US will be nonexistent.

Qualifying for loans as a foreign investor is one of the major barriers a lot of people face when coming to the US to buy real estate. Foreign investors frequently purchase property here in the US with "all-cash." There are only a handful of banks that handle these loans, but it definitely can be done. The process is no different than any other loan that is done, which includes sourcing the foreign income and documenting the foreign assets. The downside to getting this type of loan is that the lender usually doesn't want that much risk associated with the purchase, so at least 50% is required as down payment. Plus, no fixed products are offered; only fully amortized and interest-only adjustable-rate mortgage products are available. The pricing hits for this type of loan push the interest rates higher than current market rates, but it's a trade-off for being able to secure a loan without having the standard documentation required.

OK, let's say you're alright financially. Maybe even better than you thought. What's next?

KEY QUESTION #3 – DO YOU WANT TO BE A LANDLORD?

A landlord? What happened to being a real estate investor?

Relax, I'm not suddenly encouraging you to give up or think small. You can still be a real estate investor. Buying a real estate investment property solidifies that. So yes, you can and—with purchase—will be a real estate investor. Nothing's changed there.

Being a landlord only enters the picture once you own a property. At that point, as an investor, you'll also be the landlord if you choose not to employ the services of a property management team to reduce costs. Regardless of whether you choose to be the landlord or you employ a third-party property management company, understanding what it takes to manage tenants is extremely important to your success as a real estate investor. Being a landlord requires collecting rents and dealing with renters. These are hardly insignificant matters by any stretch. Do you have the patience to handle these matters, as a landlord? Patience is always a virtue, and even more so when you're a landlord. Understanding is also important since Murphy's Law seems to have a vendetta against landlords.

Murphy's Law, if you're unfamiliar with it, is the saying that "what can go wrong, will go wrong." Speaking personally, I can tell you that these words capture the essence of what it's like to be a landlord. The pipes freezing at my upstate NY duplex is an obvious example. Turnover among tenants at that property and others in my portfolio are other examples. And these are just the first that come to mind. Give me some time, and I can come up with a book-length list of all the cases where Murphy's Law has visited me as landlord. Ask any other landlord, and they'll tell you the same thing.

This is why understanding is so essential to being a successful real estate investor. You need to understand that things do happen. Pipes freeze. Tenants leave. And so much more. It's called life. Landlord life.

So, do you want to be a landlord?

Maybe you do. In that case, you'll be doing the following:

- Working together with others to solve problems regarding the property
- Communicating effectively with your tenants
- Making decisions that are in the best interests of the renters and your investment properties

- Staying in it for the long haul, especially if you're looking to create wealth

Whether you choose to be a landlord, or you employ a third-party property management team to manage the day-to-day operations of your investment, one of the most important items is effective communication with your tenants. Sadly, this seems to be the one that many landlords and property managers focus on the least. It's a shame too because your tenants are what makes everything possible. They allow you to have rental income and to be in business as a real estate investor. Knowing this, it's essential for you to be adept at communicating with your tenants. Recognize and accept that there will be times when they contact you for non-rent concerns.

It may, for example, concern a repair in their unit or some other property-related matter. Other times, your tenant may not communicate with you or the property manager. Here, they may remain silent on issues or exercise the ultimate silence, by trying to slip out without paying rent. In all of these cases, being an effective communicator will enable you to handle whatever arises. Additionally, in that latter case of a tenant trying to slip out, effective communication in advance may defuse the situation. With some communication, perhaps the tenant feels appreciated as a renter and decides to pay the rent instead. At the end of the day, tenants provide you income and having good tenant retention, less turnover, and pride of renting will ultimately boil down to effective communication.

Effective communication with tenants also sets the stage for a solid relationship, and mutual respect, to be formed. Once you've established such a relationship, you'll inevitably find your tenants easier to work with. "Problem tenants" can transform before your eyes, as if by magic, into good and even stellar tenants. Often all it takes is a better relationship. Or, more specifically, a bit more communication and thoughtfulness, so your tenants come to see you, or the property manager, as more than just a bill collector.

Sure, you do want that rent payment on the first of the month. Probably in cash too, if they'll do it. But your communication and manner with tenants should extend beyond just these matters. For, as we've said, your tenants are the ones helping you to create wealth (via their monthly rent).

I'm not a Sunday School teacher, a Rabbi, or an Imam, so far be it from me to lecture you on morality. All I'm saying is communicate and show your renters some courtesy as you do. If they call you, return their phone calls as soon as you can. If repairs are needed on the property, get the appropriate people to make the repairs. You can do those things, right?

I'd imagine you're up to the task. Still, you need to know—in advance—whether you are. It's one of the core aspects of being a landlord.

If you do want to be a landlord, there's more to consider beyond the responsibilities indicated with our bullet points above. Another of your considerations will be screening tenants. Effective screening will avoid problem tenants in the first place and give you piece of mind as an investor. This leads to our next question (key question #4)

KEY QUESTION #4 – ARE YOU WILLING TO SCREEN TENANTS FOR YOUR RENTAL PROPERTY?

Before you can answer this, you need to know what's involved.

First off, there's the "how." How exactly do you screen tenants?

You can start by using technology. We've moved away from the days when you could post a "For Rent" sign in the window or front yard of a property and get a decent tenant in no time. We're even, in many cases, past the days of simply putting advertisements in the newspaper. Signs and newspaper ads can still work today in attracting tenants. But those methods have less chance of success than in the past. And it's not a stretch to suggest that their effectiveness will only continue to decrease.

The reality today is that anyone looking to rent will probably rely on modern technology to find their property. They won't be the only ones relying on technology. You'll also use it, especially when screening tenants.

Before you use any technology, however, you must be aware of the law. I'm talking now about all of the legal issues, both with technology and in general, that come into play when screening prospective tenants. These issues should be firmly in your mind before you ever screen anyone.

The legal issues specifically include:

- How screening is done
- Housing laws (both state and federal)
- Advertising without deception

Those three bullet points above aren't meant to be a comprehensive description of the legal issues around screening tenants. I'm not an attorney, after all, and the issues have already been well-documented elsewhere. My recommendation is to read up on the screening policies related to your situation. Knowing the information beforehand can save you from potential litigation and shelling out thousands of dollars. If you're still not sure, you can shell out considerably fewer dollars now and hire an attorney who specializes in this area.

An attorney would be useful, for example, in helping you follow the policies and procedures of the Fair Housing Act, or FHA. The FHA dictates what constitutes housing discrimination. Suffice it to say it's rather important, and you must be well in line with it.

Under FHA, your screening of prospective tenants cannot be designed to, or even appear to, discriminate due to race, religion, gender, disability, sexual orientation, or a cadre of other criteria. Not that you would, of course. But enough people did in the past to make FHA the necessary and highly comprehensive law it is today.

Now, assuming you don't violate FHA or any other laws, what does a tenant screening consist of?

When it comes to tech, there are a host of great tools out there, waiting for you to use them in screening tenants. I'm not going to play favorites here, so you'll need to find for yourself the right app/website to use in your particular screening efforts.

I want to focus on what the screening consists of, on a more macroscopic level. What to look for, in other words. That way you'll have a frame to guide your screening, and you can then "geek out" with tech tools on your own time.

As you screen potential tenants, some of the fundamental things to look for include:

Employment

Where do they work, and where have they worked in the past? In general, a prospective tenant should have at least six months at the same employer.

Current Income

How much do they earn now? You can see by checking the current pay stubs a tenant has from their employer. Past pay stubs will also be helpful since they can indicate changes—often substantial ones—in a tenant's income.

Credit History

How's their credit? Does the prospective tenant pay their bills? Their credit history will tell you all the juicy details.

Previous Rental History

Where has the prospect rented in the past? And even more important, have they ever been evicted? You can get the facts here by requesting rental references (usually past landlords) and then calling them to check.

· · · · · · · · ·

You can get rental references, and much of the other information above, by having the tenant fill out an application. Make sure they complete this application in full. Anything that doesn't apply to them should be marked with a dash or N/A (not applicable).

After they've completed it, go over the application to make sure it's correctly filled out. Ask the applicant to provide you with character references, too, so these can be checked.

Then request a valid photo ID. With the ID, you'll be able to make sure that the person is who they claim to be. A driver's license works fine as ID. Take it from the client and copy the driver's license number on the application.

From here, let the prospective tenant know that you'll be doing a background check and a credit check. A good prospect won't have a problem with either. If they do have an issue with the checks, you may be looking at a potential problem renter. Prospective tenants will have to provide their consent, however, for the credit check. They can't be forced into it. Make sure the tenant is clear that they can say no to the credit check.

An in-person meeting comes next in the screening process. This is particularly important if the prospect filled out your application online, or if you haven't personally met them. I realize that in the world of modern technology, face-to-face meetings can get pushed to the back burner. However, meeting a prospect in person can show you their personality, and if they're someone you would want to rent your property to. Given the importance of tenants to your cash flow, you should have no difficulty making 30 minutes or so to meet with them.

Returning for a moment to the rental application, be sure it has a code of conduct. This code states the "rules of the road" for living at your property. It's what the tenant must adhere to should you allow them to rent from you. The code of conduct will also include what's expected of you. Having a code ensures that everyone—the prospect and you—has a clear understanding up front on the rules and expectations. It should all be explained in the code of conduct in an easily understandable manner. If you're unsure about the wording, you should seek counsel from a real estate attorney who specializes in this area.

Does that sound like a lot of work? Finding an attorney. Tackling, as well, all of the other matters related to being a real estate investor and a landlord. I'll be the first to admit that it can be a lot of work. At least initially. Which is why, for the umpteenth time, I'm adamant on the need to take stock of yourself before you begin. See everything you'll need to do and decide if you even want to do it.

While we're talking about time-intensive things, let's cover insurance.

It's a "necessary evil" for anyone in REI. Like it or not, if you're going to own property and maybe even manage it yourself, you need adequate insurance. Your property must be properly covered, with a level of insurance that's more than adequate.

Are you willing to take the time and spend the necessary money to do that?

I won't leave you hanging on this one. Let's examine it now, with our fifth key question.

KEY QUESTION #5 — ARE YOU WILLING TO PROPERLY INSURE YOUR RENTAL PROPERTY?

Part of answering this question about insurance means understanding why it's so important in the first place.

On that, I'd remind you of how Murphy's Law seems to have it out for landlords. Considering everything that can go wrong, don't go wrong yourself by purchasing a dirt-cheap insurance policy. A policy that "kinda sorta maybe" covers *some* parts of your property, but only when it's a sunny day. Go the extra mile on insurance. This means, for example, that your policy covers more than just the building itself.

Here are more essential things your policy needs to cover:

- Purposeful damages caused by tenants
- Accidental damages
- Personal and property liability
- Loss of income

Make sure you're covered on the essentials above. Then, think beyond and do your research on what else is needed. The key in all of your efforts on insurance should be to recognize that it's difficult to go too far. I'm not suggesting you need to have insurance against ghosts haunting your building or asteroids demolishing the upper floors. But it doesn't hurt to be prepared for other, more normal things. And being prepared begins with a consideration of insurance and what it would consist of in your particular case.

Feeling intimidated by this talk about insurance? I'll admit that it can intimidate and overwhelm newbies. So, too, can screening tenants and handling complex financial documents. And these are just a few of the potentially headache-inducing aspects of entering REI.

With so much "intimidating" stuff to do, is it all worthwhile? It ought to be if you're going to figuratively sweat your way through it. Like the other questions thus far, let's talk this particular question out too. That way, we can see whether all these efforts—the so-called "necessary evils" of being in REI—are worth it.

KEY QUESTION #6 — IS ALL THE EFFORT WORTH IT?

Your judgment of whether REI's "necessary evils" are worthwhile will probably be based on what you see as the payoff. What is the proverbial "pot of gold" at the end, awaiting you if you do what's necessary now? Sure, there's the "feeling of accomplishment" and all that fuzzy emotional stuff. But really, what's in it for you as a potential payoff?

Among the possible payoffs, I'd recommend looking at two, in particular: your residual income and the tax benefits.

Payoff #1 - Your residual income (How much can you make through rentals?)

Your residual income will be your cash flow, the amount of cash which "flows" to you each month from your rental properties.

At the risk of boring you with repetitive material, we can keep this part short. After all, we've already devoted large chunks of other chapters to the idea of cash flow. What I'll say on it here is purely intended to further your understanding of potential REI payoffs.

To that end, we need to know whether a property does, in fact, have a positive cash flow (i.e., if it's income-generating). This way, you'll know up front if it's going to be financially worthwhile to get involved with the property.

Sadly, you can't determine such information simply by asking the seller. Sellers have an obvious bias, and there's also the chance they don't know. The best way to get the full truth is to request the past five years' worth of bank records and expenses from the seller. If they can't pull them together or aren't willing to share them with you, get out of the deal.

If you do get the financial records from the seller, you can now calculate the property's cash flow.

Here's what you'll do:

1. Add up the income per year to get the net income.
2. Add together the expenses per year to get the property's net operating expenses.
3. Subtract the expenses from the income to obtain the property's net operating income.
4. Find the debt service fees and subtract them from the net operating income.

Now, here's an example of how you'd do it on a specific piece of property.

Example – Assessing a property's cash flow

Meet Susan. She's a real estate investor who finds a great potential property. It's a 300-square-foot condo in a prime urban location in Washington, D.C. At a price of $100,000, the condo seems like a steal by city standards.

Is it? Let's find out...

We'll begin by looking at Susan's potential payments. If she did buy the property, Susan would have a 20% down payment and then get a mortgage for the remaining $79,200. Since she had at least 20% down, Susan would not pay for personal mortgage insurance (PMI). She would, however, pay to service her debt, an annual amount of $6,403.

Since the property was for investment purposes, Susan wouldn't just be paying for it. She'd also be renting it out, having other people pay her for use of the property.

Suppose that in renting it out, Susan's first year would earn her $1,107 (a 4.5% profit). During the second year, she wouldn't have to pay the closing costs, so her earnings might increase to $5,683 (a 22.9% profit). As time went by, Susan could then increase the rent and potentially earn a 25.3% profit in the third year and a 30.6% profit in the fifth year. These earnings would, collectively, give her a five-year pretax average profit of 22.2%.

Building on our example with Susan, let's think long term. Suppose we repeat the process, working up to nine more properties, each of which is producing positive cash flow. You could potentially wind up with a positive cash flow of over $75,000 per year.

Maintaining ten properties might be a headache, though. Unlike Susan, perhaps you'd hire a maintenance man for $30,000 per year. With ten properties, you'd still be making an annual income of $45,000.

Find a deal like Susan (in our example), and you can earn some great residual income. Along with that, you might also be in a position to reap some incredible tax benefits. These benefits are the second of the potential payoffs for RE investors. Another of the reasons why going through all the supposed "headaches" could be very, very worthwhile to you in the end.

Payoff #2 – Tax Benefits (What tax benefits can you qualify for as an RE investor?)

Tax breaks can be a definite payoff in REI. Don't write off these write-offs just because you're not filthy rich and in the so-called 1%. Dig in, explore, and you may find some sizable savings on taxes from your REI efforts.

The breaks are most substantial for middle-income investors who are their own property managers. This comes from the fact that the value of tax relief depends, overall, on your annual income and what type of job you have.

It's also worth pointing out that while breaks are most significant for the middle class, tax shelters do exist for income produced by passive investors and high-income earners. Therefore, don't rule out tax shelters/breaks if you're in one of the latter two groups.

You might, for example, be able to get tax breaks from maintenance costs and marketing costs on the rental property. These two costs can be deducted from a property's income, no matter what tax bracket you're in. Besides that, you might be able to deduct other expenses, such as:

- Interest on the mortgage
- Property insurance
- Utilities
- General maintenance and repairs
- Management fees
- Marketing costs for renting the property
- Depreciation

Not bad, right? And that's just the basics. Whoever does your taxes can probably find even more ways for you personally to write off taxes on your real estate investments.

For that list of expenses (above), let me call your attention to depreciation. It ranks among the most important expenses on the list.

Having covered depreciation at length in Chapter 4, let's tread softly on it here. We'll do so by focusing on a few fundamentals and an example putting them all together.

Depreciation – A Closer Look

Simply put, depreciation is the fact that your tangible assets diminish in value over time.

A quick example would be an oven that you'd buy for a rental house. It's a safe bet that you'll need to buy a new oven in the coming years. After all, even the best ovens are bound to wear out. Therefore, the value of the oven can be claimed over a period of say five years, as a deductible expense on your taxes.

From this example, we can, therefore, view depreciation as a means of sheltering income, keeping the income from being taxed.

Depreciation goes way beyond ovens too. One way you might also use it is by depreciating the value of a rental house's structure. As the house's owner, you'd claim that the value of your rental will decrease from its purchase price, down to $0 over 27.5 years. With that claim, the annual amount would be sheltered as depreciation and potentially deducted from property income before paying taxes.

Here's a third example of depreciation. This time, we'll throw actual numbers in to make it even clearer for you.

Let's say you invest in a $500,000 house that can accommodate four different renters. You put down $100,000 on the property and then take out a mortgage on the rest. The ensuing $400,000 mortgage sits at a 7% interest rate. In dollar terms, the mortgage costs you about $2,662 in interest per month.

On top of that, you're also paying additional costs of $500 per month. The additional costs include management fees, repairs, insurance, and advertising.

At the same time, you do have money coming in. For our example, suppose your monthly rental income is $1,000 per unit. For your four-unit property, that amounts to $4,000 total. After using this income to pay your expenses, you end up with a positive cash flow of $838 per month. Annually, this would be equal to $10,056. A modest paycheck, but don't get attached to it just yet. The reason is that your $10,056 would be viewed as taxable income. At a 30% tax rate, you'd have to cut off about $3,000, ending up with approximately $7,056.

While taxes may take a bite out of your wallet, as in our example, there's still hope. You may be able to benefit from tax breaks, as we've said. This is especially true where depreciation is concerned.

To see how, consider again our example where the $10,056 was "eaten" down to just $7,056. In this case, you could keep the Tax Man from dining on your income by depreciating your building over time. Doing that would reduce the amount of taxable income you'd be required to pay taxes on.

What specifically would you do? You'd begin by subtracting out the appraised cost of the land—in our example, it's $75,000. (Land, if you'll recall from Chapter 4, doesn't depreciate).

After taking land out of the picture, you'd see that the cost of your structure is $425,000. Divide that out over 27.5 years, and you'd have an annual depreciation expense of $15,454.

$15,454 is more than $10,056, isn't it?

Which means...

...that your tax obligation on the $10,056 rental income is eliminated.

Nice, but what happened to the rest of the money? That is, where did the remaining $5,398 in depreciation expenses go?

The answer depends on your occupation and income level. If you're not a real estate professional (in the occupational sense), you probably can't claim a passive loss on rental real estate investments. The pros can sometimes do it, claiming passive losses and then using these losses to offset money earned on other rental properties. There are definite restrictions and limits on how they do it.

To keep things simple on passive losses and whether they can be written off, just remember two guidelines:

1. Real estate professionals who spend more than 750 hours per year in real estate can write off passive losses.

2. If you're not a real estate professional, and your annual income (modified, adjusted gross) is less than $100,000; you can use up to $25,000 as a write-off on any other income (non-rental) per year. To do this, you must be actively involved in the rental

business. "Actively involved" means, for example, you're the one who decides the rents and accepts tenant applications.

Will you benefit from the tax breaks for landlords and real estate investors? You can, if you decide to jump in and become involved in REI. Tax breaks should not, however, be the last question to ask yourself when deciding whether you want to do this. There's one more key question to ponder before you enter the game.

KEY QUESTION #7 – WHERE WILL YOU LIVE, IN RELATION TO YOUR INVESTMENT PROPERTY?

This question may come as a surprise to you. I've put it at the end of our list since it shouldn't be the very first item you ponder. It does need to be considered, though. When you think on this, you'll be asking yourself whether you want to be a long-distance investor or whether you'd rather live near your investments (i.e., your property).

Knowing your position here is important since it keeps you from becoming emotionally invested as you look at potential properties. In other words, you can avoid letting your desire to move impact your judgment. You won't fall into the trap of becoming attached to a lousy deal just because you can see yourself living in an idyllic location nearby it (e.g., at the beach or in the mountains). You'll avoid that by having a clear sense, in advance, of where you stand.

To help you in this regard, I recommend researching two areas to help you "divorce" your emotions. You'll then be left with the facts on whether it truly makes sense to move to a given area.

Among the areas for research, one would be tax rates. Find out what the tax rates are in the various localities within your desired region. Check out if your state or town has any tax credits, like credits for first-time home buyers, senior citizens, or veterans.

Then look at the cost of living. A Google search will bring up many online calculators to help you with this. Being aware of the cost of living will allow you to know, for instance, what it takes in Marietta, Georgia versus Oakland, California. Information of this nature will further assist you in deciding whether you want to relocate. Of the websites out there, you can start with Homefair's cost of living calculator (homefair.com/calc/salcalc.html).

After your calculations, I recommend looking at three additional items. It's only right since a move is no small thing. Look now at the following:

#1 - Schools

If the property is in a different school district and you have kids, what are the new area's schools like? Look online to gauge a district's graduation rates, SAT scores, college attendance rates, and more.

#2 - Transferring Utilities

Can you use the Internet to set up your utilities after you've moved, or transfer your existing ones?

#3 - Changing Addresses

If you're moving your primary residence, you'll need to change your address with the postal service. This entails completing an online form at www.usps.gov.

· · · · · · · · ·

That's the end of our seven key questions. If you haven't already done so, take a moment now and answer each of them for yourself. Give it some honest thought and see how you fare.

Then, once you've done that, join me in the following section.

POTENTIAL INVESTMENT DANGERS ("RED FLAGS")

Real estate investment certainly has its payoffs, as we saw earlier. Passive income. Tax benefits. Plus the pride of owning property and being an investor.

These benefits are all likely to be on your mind as you take stock of your situation. Still, you can't stop there in "reviewing the herd." To truly know whether REI is for you, you must also think about the downside. Not just the paperwork "headaches" like insurance. But also the genuine dangers of investment. These dangers include, but are certainly not limited to, financial losses and extreme emotional stress.

Fortunately, you don't have to enter REI blindly and be at the mercy of such dangers. You can avoid that by knowing in advance what to look out for.

We'll cover a few of those points, the veritable "red flags," now. Each of the following are signs that you should be aware of when considering investments. Any of them will indicate to you that an investment "opportunity" is nothing of the sort.

#1 – Incorrect information

Make sure you have the correct information regarding the property. Don't rely on the listings alone. Make phone calls and, better yet, pay a visit to the property. It may or may not look like it was described in the listing.

#2 – Less than what you want

Honestly speaking, does a given property have all that you want? Or, in your excitement to do a deal, are you settling for less?

You can answer these questions by walking through the property. If you find that it's not what you want, don't settle. You'll only end up disappointed. That said, it's OK to have a property with small repairs or upgrades to make for your first time.

#3 – Extensive work

Stay away from the rental properties that require extensive work. Otherwise, you'll have to pay large sums for repairs/upgrades or get a loan. Examples of "extensive work" would include new roofing, fixing the siding on the house, and upgrading the HVAC system. In contrast, "minor work" would include installing new carpets and resurfacing cabinets.

#4 – Steep Mortgage

"Steep" is a relative term that's going to depend on your financial state. Nonetheless, regardless of your finances, some mortgage loans will simply be more than you can afford to pay back each month. If you do require a mortgage loan for a property, you should avoid any such cases. Choose a mortgage that you can comfortably work with. This will ensure that the end of the month is just the end of the month and *not* a mad scramble to get the money to pay your mortgage.

#5 – Deals you don't fully understand

"If you don't get it, you don't get it." That's a phrase used by the *Washington Post* in their advertising campaigns. It's also a great slogan for realistically assessing investment opportunities. With potential REI properties, if you don't understand what's involved, you may want to pass.

This is particularly true for paperwork that's unclear to you. With paperwork, as with a deal in general, it's imperative that you take a "gut check." Press pause for a moment on your desire to get your first piece of real estate. Analyze all that's required, including those things you don't initially understand. When you do, you'll likely be asking questions about how the deal will affect you financially and going over everything you can find on the property. Then, after all, that, if you still don't get it, take the *Post*'s advice and "don't get it."

· · · · · · · · ·

While we're on dangers, it's only right to talk about the Internet and its role in assessing REI opportunities. After all, stories about Internet scams abound. And I was quite vocal earlier about this, with my Baltimore story.

Even with all that negativity, however, it's a mistake—at least in my opinion—to brush off the Internet for REI. There are dangers, sure, but the web can still be quite helpful in finding properties.

I, for one, am *not* opposed to relying, in part, on the Internet. I still believe there's no substitute for an in-person, "boots on the ground" investigation, but I'm no technophobe either. I recognize that some technology—especially what's online—can be an absolute godsend for RE investors. Examples would include online video tours of a home, web-based mortgage calculators, and apps enabling live chats with brokers. Each of these examples serves a valuable purpose, and I'll be the first to admit it.

Also, I tend to support, in general, most new REI-related technology. My rationale is that it gives you and I, as investors, more options. We don't have to blindly enter deals. Nor do we have to settle for less ("red flag" #2). Instead, technology serves to empower us, eliminating any sense of scarcity, ignorance, or neediness.

Nonetheless, I do think technology has its limits, especially for new RE investors. If you're starting out, I do *not* recommend buying property online, sight unseen. It's just not a good idea, even with current stats, which show approximately 3% of all online web shoppers buying real estate over the net. That's 3% of everyone making purchases of anything using the Internet. A vast number to be sure. And a figure that's expected to increase over the next five years.

Online shoppers can do as they please, but where real estate properties are concerned, I won't be joining them. You shouldn't either. Not as a new investor, and probably not any time after.

The only exception I can potentially see is when you're a seasoned veteran, with a strong record of successful REI deals and a carefully crafted team of investment partners. Under such circumstances, all of your past successes enable you to shortcut some—but certainly not all—of the prep work required on a potential deal.

If you're in this position, as a veteran, you've also taken time to build a reliable and highly knowledgeable team. Your team can, therefore, be trusted to advise you on properties. So it would not be *as much of* a stretch to consider finding a property online and then buying it, sight unseen.

Assuming it did make sense for you to buy property online, here's a look at how you'd find potential investment properties.

FINDING YOUR INVESTMENT ONLINE

Where online would you look?

A better question is where would you *not* look?

Indeed, there are thousands of different websites listing properties for sale. Much like the classifieds and the RE section of every city's newspaper, these sites provide photographs, descriptions, and pricing information. Some sites also list foreclosures, if you're interested in buying one of those as an investment.

Here are a few of the main places, online, where you can find real estate listings:

- Realtor.com

- Homestore.com

- Realestate.com

- Housebid.com

After looking online, you may have a handful of properties that you'd like to investigate further. Your next step would be to carefully research each one to get a complete picture of the properties. We've already spoken in depth on how to do that. One thing I'd add is that many towns have public listings online of property, assessed values, and past sale prices. An example, which Susan would appreciate, can be seen with the state of Maryland. (www.dat.state.md.us/sdatweb/charter.html)

Browsing such sites, you can see what a property's current owner paid for the place. If you can't find this information, you can at least see what comparable properties sold for in the vicinity.

All of that information is waiting for you, just a few clicks away. Unlike the pre-Internet days, you can find it online rather than sifting through complicated paper land records in a local town hall. If you want a field trip and the experience, perhaps you could sift through paper records. The web makes it infinitely more convenient.

· · · · · · · · ·

When you're ready, or if you'd rather finish this book first, find me in the next chapter. We'll be back in full swing, expanding your knowledge on the "what" of REI. Showing once more what you can specifically do when investing and how to do it.

For Chapter 8, that means addressing and then shattering a belief you may have on money, one that could be dramatically limiting your ability to invest, or even think about investing in real estate property. What is this limiting belief? You know what to do... Read on for more!

COMFORT CHALLENGE

This chapter was focused on taking stock of where you're at. It fits then that you do that for your network too. Following our earlier comfort challenges, you'll have chosen your market and gone to networking events. (That's a hint, by the way, if you haven't done the earlier challenges.)

Let's assume, though, that you have done all the comfort challenges up to this point. With the challenges complete, you're now in a position to begin leaning on your network.

"Leaning" isn't the same as "mooching," so make sure you're adding value to any interaction with others. The interactions, though, should also be adding value to you. You should be acquiring useful local information, finding reliable long-term people for your REI team, and perhaps even getting some intelligence on "hot deals."

Get out there now and lean on the REI network you're building. See whether the network, as it presently exists, is of any value to you.

Depending on what you find, you may need to modify your approach. Or you may find, to the contrary, that you're right on track. Regardless, you'll know. And that'll give you plenty of comfort.

★ ★ AUSSIE-ISMS ★ ★

Are there Aussies on your REI network? If so, they'll probably appreciate this chapter's Aussie-isms.

Here are a few for you to share:

- "Mad as a meat ax" – Crazy; How you'll feel if trapped in a bad real estate investment.
- "Neck oil" – Beer; Your preferred beverage if trapped in that bad investment.
- "Stone the crows" – Expression of astonishment; What you'll say when reading the next chapter of this book (hint, hint).

CHAPTER 8

US FINANCING OPTIONS

Let's talk about money. Specifically, how you get others to provide you with money for purchasing your real estate investments.

I bring up financing both to educate and to do some much-needed myth-busting. This "cash myth" runs rampant throughout the international community.

Among investors from Australia and other nations, the common belief is that US REI properties can only be purchased "all-cash." International investors consider all-cash the only option because they believe that competitive financing (i.e., financing in line with market rates) is out of reach.

Paying for a property with just your cash is great, but it means you can't maximize your leverage potential. For this reason, I'd label the all-cash and only all-cash belief as a myth. Still, as an international investor myself, I don't fault anyone for having this belief. It's certainly what I thought when I first moved to the US.

At the time, I looked at what the biggest US banks were offering and was horrified. I saw, for example, that banks would offer international investors interest rates of approximately 7–9%, with a maximum loan-to-value (LTV), aka "leverage," of 50% of purchase price. The best market rates, however, were only about 4–5% (2012-2017) and 75–85% LTV. These contrasts make sense considering that banks want international investors to have more "skin in the game," as it is harder for US banks to prove your credit score and, hence, your ability to repay the debt. The problem, though, is that international investors tend to see such contrasts and give up. We get discouraged and don't press onward in the hunt for competitive financing and leverage opportunities.

Thinking back to my early days, I might have given up too. The interest rates were certainly disheartening. There was also the credit issue. It turns out banks in the US look at your credit history using a credit score to assess whether you're a good candidate to lend to.

Coming from Australia, this concept of credit score was completely foreign to me (excuse the pun). I had no US-based credit score. In this position, like many international investors, I couldn't prove my ability to pay back debt. But US banks required me to do so before we could even talk about a loan. They didn't care, for example, that I had become a US permanent resident and acquired a social security number. They wanted to see proof—in the form of a credit score. Without one, I was essentially nonexistent to banks as a potential borrower.

I decided the credit issue wasn't going to deter me, though. Back in those early days, I took financing matters into my own hands. Once I'd found a desirable investment property, I skipped the banks altogether. Instead of trying to get a loan, I began to save up my own money.

Over about eighteen months, living in NYC no less, I saved up $45,000. As you might imagine, these were a *very* frugal eighteen months. I didn't exactly live on ramen noodles, but I did spend a whole lot less money than before. My frugality and saving allowed me to then buy a triplex in Syracuse, New York, and pay all-cash. If you have to reread that paragraph, yes! I did buy my first property for $38,000 all-cash. The barriers to entry here in the States are much lower compared to other first-world countries (like Australia, U.K., Canada, and Europe).

While I paid in cash for the Syracuse property, I didn't lose sight of the banks. In the back of my mind, I knew the day would come when the banks would recognize me and be willing to offer a loan. Moreover, I also recognized that my experiences would allow me to eventually educate other international investors about US banks and financing in general. For these reasons, I still went through the painstaking research process. I made sure to research everything.

You're about to read the result of my research. In the chapter ahead, I'll be sharing all the ways that an international investor can access some leverage to aid with their purchases. I'll also be demystifying the process of getting financing, so you can go out and do what we're talking about here.

Not an international investor? Are you, instead, an investor from the US—either a citizen or a permanent resident? In that case, I'd still advise you to read this chapter. Do the "hard work" of turning a few pages. You'll learn something new and, if nothing else, you'll be better prepared when speaking with other investors.

Let's begin now with lending and demystify that process.

DEMYSTIFYING THE LENDING PROCESS

Let me start by defining some of the common questions I'm asked by my international clients and investors:

1. "I want to buy US investment properties. Can I obtain some

financing even though I don't live in the US?"

2. "What are the requirements of those lenders who do lend to international investors?"

3. "What interest rates will I have to pay as a foreign investor?"

4. "How much down payment is required?"

5. "What are the loan terms?"

6. "How quickly can lenders close?"

All of those are important questions, and they help us to frame this discussion. From a macro point of view, I can tell you that US banks do work with international investors wanting to buy US real estate. The banks' willingness explains, for example, the interest rates I mentioned earlier.

US banks, in general, aren't opposed to working with foreign investors. It's only that, as I noted, foreign investors have less apparent "skin in the game." As a result, the banks have different requirements for lending to foreign investors.

A foreign investor seeking a loan can, for example, be required to provide their tax returns from the last five years. US banks will want to see tax returns, pay stubs, employment status, current schedule of real estate owned in your home country (or elsewhere around the world), and potentially other paperwork, too, to see that a foreign investor is trustworthy and capable of repaying their loan. Otherwise, there would be a high risk—at least to the bank—of the investor defaulting. Too high a risk, in fact, for the bank to be comfortable in providing a loan.

On the subject of banks being uncomfortable, let me give you a strategy for making banks feel at ease with you, regardless of where you're from.

I perfected this strategy in my early days with the Syracuse triplex. As I mentioned before, I bought the triplex with my own money, so no banks were involved initially. Banks only entered the picture *after* I'd made the purchase.

Following the purchase, I found a local bank in Syracuse near my property. The bank's exact name is irrelevant, but I can practically guarantee you've never heard of them. Local means local, and this particular bank was quite small. Size matters, as they say, and this was no exception.

Because of its small size, the local bank was easier to work with. I began my relationship with them by setting up an account. The account was intended as a vehicle for building my "credit" and credibility as a future potential borrower. Over the next six to seven months, I built credit by depositing rental checks from my property into the bank account. All the while, I made sure—in a genuine way—to interact with the bank's staff and form a relationship with the bank manager. These efforts made the bank comfortable with me. In time, I proved myself to the extent that I could approach the bank about obtaining a loan.

The loan became necessary because I'd run out of my investment capital and needed help to buy my second property. The bank, for its part, was happy to provide me with the loan. Despite being an American bank, it willingly did the "unthinkable," and gave me, the international investor, a business refinance loan, so I was able to release some of the equity in the first investment property to help buy investment property number two.

My experience with the local bank isn't an exception. You can employ a similar strategy if you choose. The bottom line, though, is that banks do provide market-competitive loans to foreign investors. You may have to work at it like I did, but it's possible.

The key is to think about loans from the lender's perspective. Put yourself in their shoes. Lenders (i.e., banks, credit unions, etc.) have three main concerns:

1. How much money will they make if you make all of your payments?

2. How much money will they make (or lose) if you don't default on your mortgage?

3. How do they make sure the risk of you defaulting (as a foreign investor) is extremely low, or nonexistent?

These concerns are at the forefront of most lenders' minds when assessing you and your situation. Depending on how you fare with each question, they'll decide what sort of loans to offer or not offer. Also, as a foreign investor, it's understandable that you may give slightly different answers to those questions than a US resident. Make sure that you *can* answer each question in a way that's favorable to the lender.

Lenders aren't the only ones making an assessment. We should be carefully assessing the lenders and their loans as well. When we evaluate the offerings, we'll mainly be concerned with the following:

1. Costs and payments

2. The time it takes to close the loan

3. The lender's underwriting process

4. The documents we need to provide to get them to say "yes."

Like the earlier set of questions, answering these four is equally important to any investor wanting to buy real estate as an investment vehicle.

I'd like to share some information on the types of loans offered in the

US. We'll cover some terms and concepts worth knowing, keeping it broad and not getting too bogged down in interest rates and amortization schedules (which are essential, don't get me wrong).

TRADITIONAL MORTGAGES

Traditional mortgages are the best-known type of real estate loan. This would be the classic single-family home mortgage (and its close cousin, the trust deed). The popularity of such loans can be explained by their straightforward nature. You place a down payment, typically 15–25% of the purchase price, and then get a loan for the rest of the purchase price, with the real estate serving as collateral for the loan. If you are an international investor, as I mentioned earlier, the bank will probably require you to put more skin in the game, typically 40–50% of the purchase price as a down payment.

Despite their popularity and simple nature, traditional mortgages aren't always the best choice for an investor. For starters, this category of loan usually covers single-family homes, which aren't typically the strongest assets for investors. On top of that, most institutions are reluctant to grant a mortgage to someone who already has a small handful of other mortgages. Mortgages aren't like baseball cards, where you can collect as many as you want. Instead, there are definite limits on the number of traditional mortgages you can have, especially in light of the 2008 recession.

If you do go the traditional mortgage route, you'll be dealing with either the big, cookie-cutter banks (Bank of America, TD Bank, Wells Fargo, etc.) or the local banks and credit unions. The latter (local banks and credit unions) are financial institutions focused on one part of the country. An example would be the small bank I worked with in my story about building credit and relationships with a bank. As that story indicates, it's often easier to deal with these smaller institutions.

Whoever you deal with in getting a traditional mortgage, there are four basic things to consider. These four are different from the previous four considerations (in the heading above), as this set now is focused specifically on payments and returns.

When considering these aspects of loans—whether traditional mortgages or other loan categories—here's what you should concentrate on:

1. Interest rates

Interest rates matter since they dictate how much you'll pay on the loan in interest.

2. Amortization

Amortization means the paying off of your loan on a set schedule in recurring installments over a given time frame. Look for loan terms with amortization periods of 15 years or more. In the US, you can expect to see amortization periods of 15 years, 20 years, 25 years, or 30 years. The longer the period is for repayment, the less your monthly payment is.

3. Interest-only period

If possible, see whether a bank will give you an interest-only loan for the first couple of years. Some mortgage products offer investors interest-only for the first 12–24 months. This way you'll only be required to pay interest and won't have to also pay any of the principal.

4. Loan-to-Value (LTV)

This is a ratio comprised of the loan amount compared to the value of the property that the loan is for. Banks use it to measure the risk factor on the loan. As I've said, when banks lend to international investors, they reduce their risk by making international investor put more skin in the game. The more money an investor has in any one deal, the less likelihood of default from that investor.

Let's move off mortgage types for just a moment to look at the basics of payment. Generally speaking, there are two basic payment types: fixed rate and adjustable rate.

BASICS OF PAYMENT: FIXED RATE VS. ADJUSTABLE RATE / BALLOON PAYMENTS

Loans with a fixed rate have their interest rate and regular payments set in stone. As a result, there's no mystery on paying down the loan. You get the loan money, then pay the lender a certain amount every month until you've paid back the loan and the interest. It's simple and, unsurprisingly, fixed-rate payments are associated with our first category of loan: traditional mortgages.

As an investor, fixed-rate payments may give you a measure of certainty. But you should not necessarily limit your thinking to only this first payment type. If you're willing to think creatively, and potentially have less certainty, you'll find other loan types out there, some of which could end up being more useful to you.

On a basic level, we can group some of these loan types under the category of an adjustable rate. "Adjustable rate" refers to the terms under which the loan is repaid. As the name implies, loans of this latter sort do not have their payment rates set in stone, as we saw with fixed-rate loans. With adjustable rates, lower payments may be possible at first. Then, perhaps on a schedule or after renegotiation, higher payments would be necessary, as dictated by movement in the stock market and indexes such as the LIBOR or yield on the Treasury.

So why would you consider a variable rate loan? The main reason is that it might currently have a lower rate than that of its cousin, the fixed-rate loan. If you're investing as a developer or a flipper, loans with an adjustable rate could be just the thing. You'd consider them if you're not planning to own your property for a long time. Instead, your aim would likely be to acquire property, increase its value, and then sell the property within 12 to 24 months. In this scenario, you are hedging your bets that adjustable interest rates will remain lower than a fixed-rate mortgage product over the foreseeable short term.

Nonetheless, you should still recognize that loans on adjustable payment terms entail greater risk for you, the investor. The risk is that interest rates follow the "market" and in the event interest rates spike, you'll be stuck paying a higher monthly rate compared to the fixed-rate product.

Also, just to be clear, we've been talking in this heading about the basics of payment, which apply to various types of loans. Let's return now to covering the loan types. We'll be moving beyond traditional mortgages to see what else is out there.

PORTFOLIO LOANS (BLANKET LOANS)

Portfolio or blanket loans cover multiple investment properties, which serve as collateral for the loan. This makes them attractive to both investors and banks, as the risk of default is now spread over multiple properties.

Like any loan, a portfolio loan must be paid off. The difference with portfolio loans, though, comes from the fact that payments can be creatively structured based on the holdings in an investor's portfolio. This is done by pooling together properties in a portfolio rather than addressing them individually. Pooling allows a bank or other lender to decrease the risk on the loan, since that risk is spread out over more deals. As an example, a portfolio loan could spread the risk out over three twenty-unit properties in an investor's portfolio. In this case, there would be less risk on each property.

As for actually paying portfolio loans, they usually have a "release clause." This clause allows the recipient to pay off a portion of the loan and sell off individual deals in the portfolio.

BRIDGE LOANS OR (HARD MONEY LOANS)

Need some quick cash? You might want to consider bridge loans or hard money loans. This kind of loan allows current owners of real estate to leverage their existing assets and take out new loans.

Conceptually, these loans provide a short-term "bridge" for investors. In this way, bridge loans are often used when investors want to swap real estate properties in and out of their portfolio. They'll take out a bridge loan against a current investment property, use it to buy a new property, and then sell either the original property or the second property at a profit in order to pay off the loan.

An example here would be a multifamily property that required some short-term work. A traditional loan on such a property might be difficult for you to get because a lending institution, thinking long-term, might view the loan as too risky. If, however, you pursued a bridge loan or hard money loan, it might be a different story. The latter form of loan is easier to obtain on account of its shorter time frame. You'd be looking at a loan of, say, two to five years versus twenty-five years or more (in traditional cases).

After that brief two- to five-year window, the lender would want the money back. By that point, you'd hopefully have gotten into the deal and pushed the net operating income (NOI) of your property up. You'd be in a place then to approach banks about a traditional mortgage. Banks would be more open to giving you a traditional mortgage since you'd have created value for the property. You would refinance with a traditional mortgage and use the loan proceeds to pay off the bridge loan lender.

If you want to go the bridge loan route, you'll need to find a hard money investor or local bank. This kind of investor has capital (i.e., hard money) to loan out to you. Typically, you'll find these investors and banks near the properties you want to invest in. Because they live nearby, a hard money investor knows the local market well and can easily check on their investments to make sure everything's running smoothly. (For more on hard money investors, stay tuned. We'll be looking at them in greater detail later in this chapter.)

RECOURSE & NON-RECOURSE LOANS

Recourse. Now there's a word you probably don't use every day. What does it mean?

Recourse debt holds the borrower personally liable. This means that with recourse debt (loans), lenders can collect what is owed for the debt even after they've taken collateral (home, credit cards).

Lenders won't have this ability, though, if the debt (loan) is non-recourse. All other debt falls under this second distinction and is considered non-recourse. Typically, commercial properties and loans are non-recourse and traditional mortgages for single-family houses are recourse.

Given what's at stake, it's an understatement to say you should know whether you're dealing with recourse versus non-recourse debt. The essential difference has to do with which assets a lender can go after if you as a borrower fail to repay a loan.

For both types of loans, the lender is allowed to seize any assets that were used as collateral to secure the loan. In most cases, the collateral is the asset that was purchased by the loan. For example, in both recourse and non-recourse mortgages, the lender would be able to seize and sell the asset to pay off the loan if the borrower defaulted.

The difference comes if money is still owed after the collateral is seized and sold. In a recourse mortgage, the lender could go after the borrower's other assets or sue to have his or her wages garnished. In a non-recourse mortgage, however, the lender is out of luck. If the asset in this situation does not sell for at least what the borrower owes, the lender must absorb the difference and walk away.

Hearing this, you're probably wondering why anyone would ever go with a recourse loan. After all, who in their right mind would willingly agree at the start that if they defaulted on a loan, their assets and even their wages could then be seized? It may seem crazy to you that anyone would accept such a loan.

Any craziness ends though when you consider that non-recourse loans are only applicable to commercial real estate with a minimum loan amount considered for non-recourse lending (typically $1.5 million in debt or higher). Furthermore, non-recourse loans are not an option for properties under four units. And loans of this type are reserved for individuals and businesses with the best credit.

Given all those distinctions, recourse loans aren't just *an* option, they're the only option, at least for most borrowers. Also, even if you can get a non-recourse loan, you might still want to go with a recourse loan instead. The reason is that failure to pay off a non-recourse debt may leave other assets unharmed, but your credit score will still be affected in the same way as a failure to repay a recourse debt. So you still lose.

In laymen's terms, a lender (bank) will only offer non-recourse debt on a commercial asset with a loan balance $1.5–$2 million or greater, as the asset is viewed as a business and, thus, the value of the asset is dictated by the net operating income of the property. Unlike single-family houses, or assets with four units or less, the risk of default is greater, as the occupancy of these assets will determine if the borrower can pay off the debt. Non-recourse debt isn't offered on single-family houses because if the tenant moves out, the property is 100% vacant. Therefore, the bank needs the borrower to be liable for the debt repayments. Compare this to a 100-unit commercial property; there is less risk of all 100 tenants getting up and moving out, which means there is less risk of default on the loan.

While recourse loans are an important aspect of financing, many international investors never even get to the point of considering them. This is due to the flawed assumption discussed at the start of this chapter: the assumption that if you're an international investor, your US REI properties can only be bought with all-cash. Acting on this all-cash and *only* all-cash myth, international investors often don't even look for financing, much less recourse loans.

Fortunately, not every international investor makes this mistake. Financing can still be a challenge. The challenge here is locating the right product that suits your needs. Let's solve that difficulty and further shatter the myth by explaining where you, as an international investor, can find financing.

WHERE INTERNATIONAL INVESTORS CAN FIND FINANCING

Big International Institutional Banks

These include the "big banks" I mentioned earlier in this chapter. A key difference, though, is the "international" part. Major institutions such as Goldman Sachs and HSBC are truly international, to the extent that other big banks like Bank of America aren't. Bank of

America's name might be a giveaway of their decidedly non-international nature. There's more to it.

Banks like Goldman Sachs and HSBC are international because they have special lending programs for international investors. The programs are designed specifically for international investors who own a large portfolio of real estate in their country of origin. Investors in this position can use the collateral in their foreign portfolio to obtain US-based financing. With financing secured, the international investors can then use it to buy US-based REI properties.

To have a big bank consider giving you financing in this way, you must meet two minimum requirements:

1. Your foreign real estate portfolio must have a minimum worth or equity, typically in the order of $500k to $1 mill (USD).

2. You must be able to make a minimum down payment, usually a six-figure amount.

Can you meet those requirements? Can you provide a large down payment, and do you have a large portfolio of properties in your home country? If so, America's big international institutional banks will welcome you with open arms. They may be able to offer you interest at rates competitive with current markets. Or the rates could be higher, approximately 25 to 100 basis points. Still, even in the second case, the fact remains that the banks are happy to talk with you.

If you're in this position, congratulations. You're in the top 1% when it comes to international investors.

Among your options as an elite international investor, I'd recommend checking out HSBC Premier. You might also turn to Goldman Sachs, especially if you're an ultra-high net worth individual and already have an account with them in your home country. If so, you'd simply talk to your current client relationship officer.

Small Local Banks

Don't have a Goldman Sachs account? Not in that 1% of international investors?

Not a problem. The Goldmans and HSBCs won't consider you, but maybe the small local banks will. We've already seen, for example, how I was able to work with a smaller, locally-based bank. Perhaps you could do the same.

If you choose to approach a local bank or even a credit union, you should recognize that their lending requirements to foreign investors will be different. Here's what you can expect:

1. Down payment

As a down payment, you'll usually be required to provide 40–50%. As I've mentioned earlier, the rationale for such a large down payment is that it shows the local bank/credit union that you're less likely to default. After all, you've got nearly half (40–50%) of your capital in the deal. That's some serious skin in the game.

2. Interest rates

The interest rates you're offered by the local banks and credit unions will usually be 100 to 200 basis points above the market rates (6–9%).

3. Loan terms

Expect the loan to be set at 20–30 years amortization.

4. Employment and capital reserves

As we noted earlier, international investors must figuratively jump through more hoops than their US-based counterparts. In the context of local banks and credit unions, your hoops will involve verifying your employment.

You'll also need to meet certain capital reserve requirements. These reserves typically come from opening and maintaining an account at the bank where you wish to get a loan. In most cases, you'll need to have excess cash sitting in that bank account equivalent to six months of interest payments.

If opening an account of this sort for six months with a local bank sounds familiar, it should. This was what I did with my local bank. Follow my lead on this, even if your local bank is lax on account requirements. Take the initiative, open an account with your local bank, and then hold cash reserves in it. By doing this, you'll further convince the bank that you do indeed have skin in the game.

· · · · · · · · ·

Can you meet the requirements above for local banks/credit unions? If so, you can expect the overall process to take upwards of 90 days or longer, depending on the bank.

While we're talking about banks, let me extend an invitation to you. If you'd like some more guidance on finding and working with small banks, feel free to contact me. Send me an email (info@reedgoossens. com), and I'll be happy to share some insights and provide you a referral. It's only natural since I work with a lot of smaller banks that offer financing programs to international investors. (Besides, I can't give away all my secrets in this book!)

Then again, maybe you need financing sooner. Maybe this whole 90 days or longer thing just isn't for you. In that case, you might look for your financing with hard money lenders (private lenders). To keep our discussion from being repetitive, let's go beyond just the basics we talked about before. We'll look now at the actual "nitty gritty" of approaching and working with a hard money lender.

Hard Money Lenders (Private Money Lenders)

Despite having the word "hard" in their name, working with a hard money lender doesn't have to be difficult. Not if you know what to do.

You can start by understanding where to find them. As we said earlier, hard money lenders tend to be local to the area where an investment property is situated. They want to be near the property and able to drive or even walk over to occasionally check in. Being local also makes hard money lenders well-versed in local real estate trends, including which neighborhoods are "good" versus "bad."

When a hard money lender agrees to loan you money, they'll usually do it through a short-term loan. Their loan, in turn, will be secured by the real estate you're using the loan to purchase.

Also, while we've implied that a hard money lender is an individual, it's important to understand that you may be working with multiple people. Your hard money lender may be a group of private investors, or those operating an investment fund.

Regardless of whether it's an individual or several people, hard money lenders can offer you as an international investor two unique advantages:

1. Loans are asset-based

The advantage here is that the lender will look more at the asset you're planning to buy than at you as the borrower. You'll still need to apply as a borrower, but the amount of personal scrutiny on you will be less.

2. Fast action

Hard money lenders can act very quickly—usually within two to three weeks. Their speed easily exceeds that of traditional institutions (banks, credit unions), which as we've seen, can take 90 days or more for a loan.

· · · · · · · · ·

Given their advantages, you're probably wondering what the drawbacks of working with hard money lenders are. One would be the interest rates. With a hard money lender, you're typically looking at an interest rate on your loan of 9–14%. Your loan also won't be nearly as long as with other types of lenders. Unlike the others, a hard money loan usually lasts for only twelve to eighteen months. After that period, a hard money loan can potentially be extended in six-month to twelve-month increments.

Another possible drawback of hard money loans is the down payment. You can expect to put down between 25% and 35%, depending on the condition of the asset.

Knowing their benefits and drawbacks, what do you think of hard money loans? Are they for you? Or are you turned off by the drawbacks, especially those steep interest rates?

Let me offer my insights and give you some more clarity. In my opinion, a hard money loan could make sense for you if you plan to buy an investment property (either residential or commercial) and then renovate it. In this case, your goal would be to make the renovations and thus add value to the property.

If that was your aim, you could take a hard money loan for the first twelve months while you rehabbed the property (or stabilized your asset). Once you'd added value to the property/asset, you could then get a conventional loan from a local bank and pay off the hard money loan with debt at a lower interest rate. This idea of "juggling loans" was touched on earlier in our chapter, but I want to go a step further now.

I want to emphasize the importance of not rushing haphazardly into this idea. Loans are serious business, and even more so in this case, where you'd be dealing with multiple loans. As such, I would strongly encourage you to think carefully before juggling a hard money loan with a traditional loan. This strategy should only be used if you're confident that the future value of the property, once rehabbed, will be significant enough to refinance and pay off the hard money.

Think carefully about that and be sure to also seek advice from others. Consult local real estate investors and brokers within the target market. With their advice, you can come to a better understanding of trends, pricing, and whether you'll be able to juggle the loans as you envision.

Not sold on hard money loans? Still want to shop around and see what else is out there for financing your real estate investments? Then you might like this next option.

Seller Financing (Creative Financing)

Among all the options for financing, seller financing is easily one of my favorites. I'm drawn to it, as you might be, by the fact that seller financing entails being creative. Unlike banks, credit unions, and perhaps even hard money lenders, seller financing lacks any rigidity. You're free to create a financing arrangement on your terms and based on your creative thinking.

Whatever financing arrangement you create will be negotiated directly with the seller of a property you want to purchase. You and the seller will work out everything together, from the down payment to the loan period, and all of the other "rules of the road." If you and the seller can get "on the same page" for the financing arrangements, the entire process can happen very quickly. This is because you'll be free of the red tape that usually comes when working with banks. In fact, with this scenario, the seller becomes the bank since they have considerable equity in their property.

Seller financing certainly benefits you, but what about the seller? Here, we see two major issues/drawbacks for the seller:

1. Trust

Can the seller trust you? They need to be confident that you as the new borrower will pay back the debt, particularly if you're an international investor.

All the same, if the seller has owned an income-producing property for some time, they will know its earning potential. This knowledge can make them more open to the idea of seller carry back financing (SCBF).

2. Payments over time

With seller financing, the seller doesn't get full payment when the sale is closed. Instead, they get to collect payments with interest over time. Depending on the seller, they'll either see this as a negative or a positive.

The negative would be that the seller isn't getting a lump sum payday. The positive, though, is that the financing creates a great income stream for the seller over the life of the loan.

· · · · · · · · ·

If seller financing interests you and you're in contact with a seller, my advice would be to ask them about it. The "how" and "when" of asking can be a tricky matter, but if you don't ask the question, you'll never know. This is why I always ask the seller directly if they've even considered doing seller financing (SCBF). If they haven't, I'd explain the benefits like those mentioned above.

Also, where seller financing is concerned, the importance of trust cannot be understated. As we said, trust can be regarded as a potential downside to sellers. This is why you, as the borrower, need to establish credibility with the seller. That means doing a down payment and having excess capital on hand to complete rehab/repositioning the property. It also means that you supply proof of your ability to own and operate the property from afar, along with evidence that you've established a local team.

Go the extra mile, really, in providing proof that you're up to the task. But recognize that, apart from being honest and trustworthy, everything else is negotiable and that's the beauty of seller financing.

> *TIP: Not all sellers are educated on this type of financing. If you want to learn more, including how to educate your sellers and implement this purchasing strategy, check out all my podcast episodes.*

Partner with a US-based Investor

Last but not least among our financing options is the option to partner with a local US-based investor. As options go, there are many benefits here:

1. More competitive financing — You can leverage the credit score of the local investor to obtain more competitive financing.

2. "Boots on the ground" — You gain a partner who's knowledgeable in the market and has "boots on the ground" (i.e., physically there.)

3. Less work in financing and purchasing — Your stateside partner, the US-based investor, coordinates the financing and purchasing for you.

4. Skip the "hoops" — The US-based investor you've partnered with does the pre-approval work. This means you don't have to jump through all the hoops to get pre-approved.

· · · · · · · · · ·

Given those benefits, forming partnerships with a stateside investor can be a very attractive option for financing. Perhaps even more attractive than the other financing options we've covered.

Still, as with the earlier options, don't rush. In the case of this financing option (stateside investor partnerships), you need to take care in vetting the people you consider partnering with. Ask them for references, including any previous deals they've completed successfully. You'll want to see that they have skin in the game as well.

Speaking personally on partnerships, I can say that they've been instrumental to my success. In my early years, I built my credibility as an investor by partnering with US-based investors—especially my mentors—and riding their "coattails" to successful deals. With these successes, I could then build a track record and prove my trustworthiness to other investors to partner with me and complete even more deals.

In the process of doing partnerships, I've certainly learned a lot. I've learned, for example, how difficult it can be for us international investors to obtain competitive financing. And I've learned about the overwhelming need that we have for an alternative.

Thankfully, an alternative does exist. It's in partnerships—specifically with co-investing. As a co-investor/partner with one or more US real estate investors, the international investor can then buy US real estate more easily and with more opportunities (financing, expertise, etc.) than would otherwise be possible. The exact name for this process is *"investment syndication."*

How does it work?

That's for our next chapter, Chapter 9. We'll be covering "syndication" then, in all its juicy details. Read on for a look at syndication, the best financing option that you've never heard of.

COMFORT CHALLENGE

Our comfort challenge in this chapter is designed to help you shatter your limiting beliefs on financing. I want you to see what's out there, rather than assuming you know and letting those assumptions blind you.

To complete the challenge, reach out to the local banks and big institutional banks in your area. Determine what these banks will offer to you as a borrower. Be sure to shop around and take note of pertinent details like interest rates and down payment requirements.

As you interact with the banks, compare their offerings and requirements with where you are. This means you'll be looking again at the items from Chapter 7, especially your finances and credit score. Reviewing those items now, alongside actual information from the banks, will give you a clearer and more realistic picture of where you stand on financing in the traditional sense.

★★ AUSSIE-ISMS ★★

With all this talk about banks and financing, you might be wondering what, if any, Aussie slang we could cover here. Sadly, Aussie Slang has yet to include such financing-related terms as "Porlos" (for portfolio loans) or "Hardees" (for hard money lenders). So we'll have to settle in this chapter for slang like the following:

1. "On Struggle Street" – To be struggling financially

2. "Have a lend of" – Being taken advantage of; What shady lenders do

3. "Barrack" – To cheer on; Not America's former president

CHAPTER 9

SYNDICATION BASICS

Strength in numbers.

It's a good phrase to keep in your mind as a real estate investor. The reason is that it's applicable to many of the lessons you've learned earlier in this book.

You'll find, for example, that there's "strength in numbers" when choosing your market to invest in. This is because you can be confident on having chosen the right market after you've crunched the numbers on a high number of deals in that market. There's also "strength in numbers" where deals are concerned, since the more you're involved in, the easier it is to do them. On this latter point, we've seen that being "involved in" deals is easier than you'd expect too, since you can "coat-tail" on larger deals with more experienced investors.

It's that second case (coat-tailing) that I want to talk about in this chapter. We'll expand it here, to gain a complete understanding of how RE investors collaborate. As we do, we'll see how there is definitely "strength in numbers," with "numbers" now being in a human sense (i.e., groups).

GROUNDWORK

In talking about collaboration, let's begin by laying the groundwork, getting a foundation as to what it is and why it's so important.

First, the "what." When I say "collaborate," I'm specifically referring to *"real estate syndication."* Real estate syndication is a way for investors to pool their financial and intellectual resources to invest in projects and properties much bigger than they could afford or manage on their own.

In this way, syndication helps you overcome whatever personal limitations you face as an investor. These limitations, faced by both new and seasoned investors, often include the following:

- No capital ("I don't have the capital to get into real estate")
- No time ("I don't have time to find cracking deals")
- No savings ("Once I have saved enough money I will do my first deal")
- No experience ("I don't have enough experience to get started")

Do any of those limitations apply to you? I ask because, time and again, I hear new and aspiring investors speak of limitations like the ones above. Call me harsh, but I believe those "limitations" are just excuses. Excuses made by people who don't know that REI is all about **leverage**. Open your mind to this idea of *leverage* and you'll find it possible to use other people's abilities, skills and even capital to get involved in more real estate deals.

As for your own involvement, there are two broad ways to do it. You can be involved as either an *active investor* or a *passive investor*.

Let's cover each of those now, so you can get a sense of what they entail. In doing so, I'd advise you to keep in mind the question of time.

Ask yourself how much time you can realistically dedicate to finding, analyzing, and running an investment? If you're like most people, you're probably quite busy. For that reason, being a passive investor may be your best option. Still, in order to make an informed decision, you should be aware of what it means to be involved in each way.

OPTION #1 – ACTIVE INVESTOR

Active means active. No question. If you're an active investor, you'll need to actively educate yourself on a litany of things. Those items include: finding and analyzing deals, financing, closing/due diligence, and knowing when to walk away versus when to "pull the trigger." You'll also need an active working knowledge of operating deals.

Such knowledge will indeed be power, and it's essential for anyone wishing to be an active investor. Yet educating yourself on all of those items (above) takes time. You'll be required to devote a large portion of time to learning and then applying your knowledge in the execution of deals.

Is it worth it? You'll be the judge of that. I can tell you, though, that the larger the deal, the greater the economy of scale. This in turn leads to more cash flow.

At the same time, though, larger deals also entail more responsibility on your part. If you're involved in such deals as an active investor, you'll need to handle not only the deal itself but also subsequent matters like managing and overseeing the property managers, asset managing the overall deal, and allocating dollars to certain building improvements that will ultimately lead to increased revenue. All of these things will be your responsibility. It's serious business, especially when you're at the multi-million-dollar level.

Thankfully, though, you don't need to carry all that responsibility on just your own shoulders. You'll still need to treat it as serious business, but you can offset some of the responsibility by partnering with other active investors. You can lighten the load, so to speak, and ensure nothing falls through the cracks. I often see investors collaborate in such a manner, bringing their capital together to take down a larger commercial real estate deal. This is known as syndication. It's an integral part of both active investing and passive investing.

OPTION #2 - PASSIVE INVESTOR

Being a passive investor could be your best bet if you wish to pursue REI yet still maintain your current lifestyle. You might be drawn to passive investing, for example, if you're a busy working professional and you want to get your money working for you besides investing in the stock market. You're well aware of the importance of investing and you see REI as the ideal avenue to help you achieve your financial income goals. Yet with your workload, you lack the time or the energy to find great investment deals yourself. For this reason, you'd choose to participate in commercial real estate deals as a passive investor. In this role, you bring equity (capital) to the table in exchange for owning a portion of the deal ("*co-investing*" or "*co-owner*").

Such a partnership reflects the other side of "syndication." Where you, yourself, are not in the active investor role. Rather than being active and "hands on" with the deal, you take a passive stance, simply being the one bringing capital.

As an analogy, think about a party. This can help you get clear on the difference between active versus passive investors in a syndication. In our party analogy, active investors are the organizers of the party. They're renting the party room, lining up entertainment, handling guests, and much more. Passive investors, on the other hand, are analogous to those guests who attend the party and enjoy what the organizers have worked hard to facilitate—a "good time." Guests aren't involved in the organization, nor are they involved with running the party, making sure everyone is enjoying themselves or cleaning up once people have gone home for the evening. Catch the difference? Both groups (the organizers and the contributing guests) are instrumental in making the party a success. Yet one group (the organizers) is clearly more active in facilitating the event.

From that analogy, we can see active and passive investors collaborating on a syndication in comparable fashion.

SYNDICATION – AN OVERVIEW

Like we've said, syndication means pooling money and resources together in a real estate partnership. Expanding that concept, we see it happening specifically when investors gather their money together and partner with a private real estate business. When this happens, the buying power of the group as a whole is increased.

With more capital, it's possible for those involved to acquire larger deals. This is how, for example, I was able to do those massive deals in Houston, Texas. Deals which I might, in theory, have never been involved in given my part-time approach to REI and (at the time) my novice status. Being aware of syndication, I knew better than to let these "limitations" stop me. I could confidently overcome the apparent obstacles and became a part of the "big" deals—those worth $10 million, $20 million, and up.

In my case, when I was starting out as an investor, syndication proved a definite "win." I could play in the so-called "big leagues," reaping the rewards of large deals while retaining my part-time investor status but also learning the "ropes" of the syndication business. Syndication was—and is, generally speaking—a win for the other side, one or more private real estate companies, too. These companies partner with investors in a syndication. Starting out my career as a passive investor helped me develop the confidence and knowledge to be able to transition quickly from a passive investor to an active syndicator. Over the years of investing here in the US, I have been able to start my own real estate syndication business, which has enabled me to help and partner with my own network of investors.

Looking at the other side of the syndication "coin," companies engaged in real estate syndication work at finding and sourcing great investment opportunities. Real estate syndication companies can also provide well-established teams to operate these properties after a deal has closed. In return for their efforts, private RE firms receive from investors the equity necessary to close on deals. It's a fair trade since investors want to place their money into an investment that will reap a solid return on their investment, and real estate syndication companies supply the deals to provide that return. It's also, as we've said, a definite win for both parties and the ultimate leverage opportunity.

But what side of the "win" do you want to be on? It's worth considering because all "wins" are *not* created equal. What I mean is that your winnings/gains in a syndication vary, depending on how you're involved, as either an active or passive investor. Before you can decide, it's necessary to probe deeper into the specifics of being an active versus passive investor in a syndication. So far, we've covered each in general, enabling you to get a conceptual sense. Now, though, we'll zoom in on each side, examining what they entail in practice.

SYNDICATION IN PRACTICE – FOR THE ACTIVE INVESTOR (AKA SYNDICATOR)

Mindset

If you want to be on this side of the "win," as an active investor, begin with mindset. Put this item first and foremost on your agenda. Before you can go out and raise capital from others, you need to raise your own "personal capital"—your sense of self-worth and the confidence you have in your own abilities to find and operate crackin' deals.

Depending on where you're at with either of these items, you may need to figuratively raise some serious capital. Otherwise you'll be ill-equipped to go out and raise actual capital (i.e., money). Inner doubts are likely to crush you well before you can ever pitch investors. Or if you do make it that far, you can expect the doubts to wreck any presentation you make and prevent you from rising again.

Whatever doubts you feel about raising capital from investors, acknowledge them and then work at overcoming them. When you do, you'll find it *easier* to raise $1 million, for example, on a $4 million syndication deal. I say "easier" because it still isn't easy. When I first started out raising money I thought it would be "easy," but I quickly learned the hard way that successfully raising money takes time, it takes credibility, and most importantly, it takes teamwork.

How do you work on your mindset? One of the best ways is to recognize what you bring to the table. As an active investor, you're providing a conduit between people who have capital and crackin' deals that will produce a solid ROI (Return on Investment). So it's not like you're just getting a "handout." No, you are offering investors an opportunity to place their capital into a hard asset, backed by real estate, to receive solid returns. Better returns than other investment vehicles out there (stocks, bonds, mutual funds). Get clear on this and it'll work wonders in allowing you to develop a winning mindset. (**I'd also encourage you–if you haven't–to do all of the comfort challenges in this book. They aren't called *comfort* challenges for nothing!)

Growth (Scaling)

You probably get it by now that working on yourself, mentally, is as important as working on a deal. What's also important is to keep a sense of perspective. Understand why you're even raising money in the first place.

So, why *are* you raising money? It's simple really. You're raising money in order to scale your REI business over the long term. Outside money is needed because your own capital for investing will eventually run out. When it does, you won't be able to continue growing. Your business will have figuratively hit a "ceiling," beyond which any forward growth/progress just isn't possible.

I found this out, for example, with buying duplexes in upstate New York. Like I mentioned in the chapter on financing, I eventually ran out of my own capital. In that particular case, I went to the bank and acquired a loan.

The loan, while helpful, was nowhere near the level needed to continue to scale my investing business and participate in multi-million-dollar deals. At the time, it was fine since I had yet to be involved in deals of that size. But I knew that the day was coming when I would be and that, when the day arrived, my small local bank wouldn't loan me anything close to a million dollars.

Frankly, few, if any banks, would. Not to a relatively new RE investor and especially an international one. For this reason, I had to eventually "level up" and move beyond banks into syndication, where I could begin raising my own capital from others. Only then did I gain the capital necessary to truly scale my venture (RSN Property Group) and take RSN beyond the duplexes to the point where we could be active in multi-million-dollar deals.

Let my example be instructive in your own case. It's ringing proof of how you can "level up" too. In a similar manner, you can use syndication to scale your own business and reach a place where the "sky's the limit" on the kind of deals you can be active in. To reach that level, it's necessary, as we've said, to maintain perspective.

Teamwork

Keeping things in perspective also means recognizing the important roles that other people play in a syndication. For this reason, I encourage you to see syndication as a team sport. It's analogous to being on a football team. That's "football" in both the Aussie and American sense. Regardless of whether we're talking about soccer or the "real" football, teamwork is of paramount importance.

Soccer legend David Beckham, for instance, would be nothing without a strong team behind him. Neither would Aussie football legend Tim Cahill. Both players can only reach their goals, literally, with teamwork. The same holds for you in working towards your goals in real estate. If you want to score, and do so repeatedly in REI, you need a strong team. That means developing a network of trusted professionals, as we saw in our "Team building" mini chapter. And, in the context of this chapter, it means creating a team of investors— syndication, in other words.

The result of teams in syndication is that it creates leverage. You move past your own finances and gain access to OPM (other people's money). This is a tremendous position to be in as a business owner, since the possibilities with OPM are unlimited.

Yet the money doesn't come for nothing. What specifically is required of you? Here's the "fine print," if you will, a set of some specific requirements you'll need to meet as an active investor. (*Note: our list here excludes, of course, any unique details in/around a particular deal you do.)

- Access to Deals – You must have access to deals that will provide a strong ROI for everyone involved.

- Track Record – You need a well-established track record of sourcing great investment opportunities.

- An Experienced Team – Anyone you approach for partnering in a syndication will want to see that you've got an experienced team to manage the acquisitions and operation process.

- Debt Financing – Can you provide all the debt financing to close on the deal? It's your responsibility if you're an active investor.

- Property Management – Can you or those in your network oversee the day-to-day management of a property, once the deal closes?

- Negotiations – You'll need to handle all the negations with the seller of the property. Are you up to the task?

- Legal Paperwork – It's your responsibility to provide all of it. As in *all* of it, not just a few forms, but the "whole nine yards" as they say.

- Personal Equity – While you're going to others for money, don't forget to have your own equity invested in the deal. Investors you approach will want to see that you also have "skin in the game."

Beyond this list, I'd also add some personal items. These extend beyond just mindset and require you, as an active investor, to be:

- Personable – Can you interact with others, putting others at ease and leading investor meetings?

- Knowledgeable – You need to know your material, having a clear sense of both REI overall and the property for each deal you do.

- Professional – Being professional means you're on time for meetings and have a serious manner in all other interactions with prospective syndication partners.

- Pitch-conscious – How's your elevator pitch? If you're pitch-conscious, you'll have a polished elevator pitch that you can deliver to prospective investors. Those who hear you pitch will then easily understand why you deserve capital.

- Patient – You need to have patience on your first deal(s), understanding that you may not raise boatloads of capital initially. And knowing too, that you may need to approach fifty or more people. Often well over that figure too.

Now let's look at the other side of this. The other party who "wins" in the win-win created by syndication. We'll move on here to examine, in greater depth, syndication in practice as it will apply to you if you choose to be a passive investor.

SYNDICATION IN PRACTICE – FOR THE PASSIVE INVESTOR

Does being a passive investor make sense for you? It could if you're looking to let others do the "heavy lifting" in deals. Passive investors get to sit back on large deals, ones which are "out of their league," while the active investors do most of the deal. Nonetheless, passive investors are not "bench warmers," to use our team sport analogy. You can hardly call them that, since it's the passive investor's money that allows the deal to close. Without such capital, any work by the active investors would be in vain. It's only because they contribute the necessary funds that a deal can close. So passive investors in a syndication are perfectly deserving of their check. They've earned whatever money is in that check, which is paid as a portion of the cash flow on a property.

If you like the sound of this so far, let me remind you of some other benefits to passive investors in a syndication. These would include: reduced taxable income, depreciation, cash flow, and appreciation.

In return for these benefits, your responsibility is simply to provide the down payment (i.e., investment). Depending on your individual situation with a particular deal, you may be required as well to provide some minor items. I mention this as the particulars of individual deals can vary. Still, overall, passive investors in a syndication aren't usually expected to do much—if anything—more than simply giving the funding. That's typically all you must bring to the table in order to receive a good ROI, the kind of ROI well beyond a bank's measly 0.25% per year (on a CD) and at heights of often 7–8% cash-on-cash per year—or more!

To reach those levels involves working with others in a syndication. Thus far, we've covered the "people" side of this, looking at active and passive investors. Next, let's look at the legal side. We'll talk here about how a syndication is structured.

SYNDICATION STRUCTURE

Remember LLCs? We spoke of them "centuries ago," back in Chapter 4. LLCs are just as relevant now, though, when discussing the ways a syndication can be structured. In the context of syndication, we find LLCs joined by three other types of entity structure. These four, collectively, are the means by which partners in a syndication can take ownership of a property.

1. Limited Liability Company (LLC)

2. Limited Partnerships (LP)

3. Delaware Statutory Trust (DST)

4. Tenant in Common (TIC)

On this list, the first two (LLC and LP) are at the top of the list precisely because of how common they are. LLCs and LPs are definitely the way most syndications are structured.

From experience, I can tell you that ownership of an entity is usually split up in the following way. Passive investors (aka Limited Partners – LP) are on one side with 70–75% ownership. The remaining 25–30% of ownership is then held by private real estate companies (aka general partners – GP).

Under this arrangement, passive investors buy shares in the entity that owns the property. In return, they receive three documents:

1. A subscription agreement

2. The entity operating agreement

3. A private placement memorandum (PPM)

The subscription agreement outlines what one share of the LLC is worth. The entity operating agreement indicates how the entity will be run. In describing that, the entity operating agreement works in tandem with the PPM.

The PPM, for its parts, outlines such essentials as:

- Potential risks

- How risks will be mitigated

- How the property will be operated

- Taxation

- Reporting (to the investors involved)
- Where the entity will be based
- Backgrounds of the general partners involved
- ...and much, much more

If it's helpful, you can think of a PPM as the A to Z document explaining the ins and outs of the deal and the way it's structured.

You should also realize that the PPM isn't optional. This document is required by law and must be provided to all investors participating in a private equity raise (i.e., a deal). For this reason, no credible syndication can operate without one.

Knowing that, you should consider it a deal-breaker if you're looking at a deal and those involved can't produce a PPM. In that case, I'd strongly recommend against participating in the deal. Do yourself a favor and walk away. Have the confidence to know that there *will* be other syndication deals in the future. Better deals, where those involved can readily produce a PPM.

Speaking of PPMs, you're probably curious about what one looks like. If you'd like to see a sample, I'm happy to furnish a copy. As usual, just email me (Reed@ReedsBook.com). That said, it bears repeating that I'm not a lawyer. So while I can send you a sample PPM, what I provide and my thoughts here are no substitute for actual legal advice. Accordingly, if you're thinking of investing in a syndication, make sure to have all the documentation reviewed by a lawyer.

COMPENSATION STRUCTURE

How much can you expect to earn in a syndication deal? That's going to depend to an extent on the individual deal, as each syndication has its own compensation structure. But you can get a basic sense of earnings by understanding the three fees typically found in syndication deals:

1. Acquisition fee

The acquisition fee is a one-time fee that's paid to the general partners (GP) in a syndication. It's their compensation for having taken the time to put the deal together. The acquisition fee is meant to compensate the general partners for having done such time-intensive tasks as: finding/evaluating potential deals, vetting the property manager, negotiating with the seller, carrying out due diligence, and securing lending/debt financing. For their efforts, the general partners receive an acquisition fee that's typically between 1% and 5%.

2. Asset management fee

An asset management fee is an ongoing fee paid to the GP for ongoing duties in and around the deal. These duties include: overseeing the day-to-day management of the property, establishing and implementing a capital improvement plan, reporting and maintaining distributions to the partners, and overseeing market trends to identify the most opportune time to implement a liquidity event. As for the fee itself, I've seen it charged as either a percent of the total asset value (1%), or as 2% of the gross rental income, paid out quarterly with distributions.

3. Waterfall structure

"Waterfall" and "syndication" aren't exactly words you'd expect to find in the same sentence. Still, apart from semantics, there's nothing strange or complicated about fees on the waterfall structure. It's a performance-based return to the private real estate firm for results of higher IRR (internal rate of return). This fee is paid when the GP are doing their job well and the IRR of the property increases. As the IRR hits different thresholds, the equity ownership will change, resulting in the payment of higher fees to the GP.

As an example, for returns up to and including 15% IRR, the equity ownership could be structured as 70/30. Then, if the IRR became more than 15%—say in the range of 16% to 18%—the split might change to 60/40. And if returns ultimately reached 20%, the split might then rise again to 50/50.

From our example, you can see the benefit of fees on a waterfall structure. When this structure is in place, it incentivizes a syndicator and ensures they perform well. After all, the better they perform, the more ownership and compensation the syndicator receives. Talk about strong motivation!

· · · · · · · · ·

Interested in syndication? Or perhaps you're still in the exploratory phase, wanting to know more. Regardless of where you're at, I'd encourage you to at least understand the basics of syndication. Knowledge of the basics will be profoundly helpful to you as you decide whether to be an active or passive investor.

To further your understanding of syndication, check out the miniseries I've created on my podcast. It'll walk you through the basics, along with how syndication can help scale your business and what the legal requirements are to raising capital. Below are links that will take you to the two episodes in the miniseries:

- RG 017 – What is Real Estate Syndication: Part 1
- RG 018 – Syndication Basics Part 2: How to Scale Your Real Estate Business with John Cohen
- RG 019 – Syndication Basics Part 3 - How to Raise Capital Legally with Mark Roderick

Along with those links (above), let me also leave you with a preview of our next chapter. Having wrapped up our look at syndication, we're going to be entering new territory in the coming pages. Our topic for Chapter 10 is easily among the most important ones yet. We'll be looking at what it means to actually close a deal, covering everything that's required, from due diligence to negotiating to that final moment, when you must decide whether or not to "pull the trigger" and commit yourself to the deal. When that moment does come, will you be ready? Read Chapter 10 to ensure you are.

COMFORT CHALLENGE

Nothing fancy here. This comfort challenge won't require you to do any soul searching. Nor will you need to crunch numbers in a spreadsheet or do extensive web research. We're keeping it nice and simple this time around. Your comfort challenge here is merely to download a short e-book I've written, entitled *The Art & Science of Raising Capital Like A PRO – The 4P Rule*. You'll find the e-book at www.reedgoossens.com/books

Once you've read the e-book, you'll be able to start creating your pitch deck. This deck, if you'll recall, is the set of materials you'll be using when pitching investors. Having such a deck is important since it establishes— in your own mind and for those you meet—what your position is. What do you bring to the table, in other words, that would make it worthwhile for someone to invest in a syndication deal with you? With a pitch deck, this question can be clearly answered and illustrated to everyone you meet. It'll also give your personal clarity about who you are and the types of investment opportunities you can realistically pursue.

★★ AUSSIE SLANG ★★

In our last slang section (for Chapter 8), we joked about made-up "Aussie-isms," those pretend terms that Australians *could* use as slang for real estate financing matters. For this chapter, we'll need to continue that thread, since Aussie slang is similarly devoid of terms for RE syndication.

Us Aussies may not have slang for syndication, but if we *did*, my guess is that it might resemble the following:

1. "Teamer" — Syndication; Since it's a team sport
2. "Subie" — A subscription agreement
3. "Tell-all"— A PPM

CHAPTER 10

THE CLOSING PROCESS

"Your net worth is directly proportional to your network."
– As said by many a business guru

Math won't save you. Not from becoming involved in a bad deal.

You can do all the computations you want and still be horribly wrong.

The same goes for market comps and analysis.

You can pull comps and analyze them to your heart's content...only to find later that your efforts failed to uncover the truth about a property.

Worst of all—sometimes even an in-person visit won't be enough.

You can visit a potential investment property, find nothing noticeably wrong with it, and then end up in a deal you despise.

Now, in saying all this, my point isn't to scare you away from doing deals.

Nor am I trying to make the point that calculations, market comps/ analysis, and visiting a property aren't important. All of them are and you must do each of them, whenever you consider a potential deal.

And, I'm also not implying the need to just have faith. As in doing what you can and then accepting that "whatever will be, will be." Or that the deal's "in God's hands now," so you just need to do it and trust that everything will work out.

What then am I getting at?

What's the point in all of these warnings?

The idea is that there's more to assessing an investment property than what we've covered thus far.

There's another layer to it. Another step, if you will, in the "recipe" for successful REI here in the US.

Fortunately, this step is usually the last one before you can "pull the trigger" on a deal—handing over the money and getting the deed to the property.

So it's not like you're light-years away from ever being able to actually do the deal.

No, you're close. Really close!

But you're not quite there yet.

This last step remains.

DUE DILIGENCE

Or "true diligence," as we might *unofficially* call it. Since this is where you gain the truest sense of a property that you possibly can.

Due diligence finds the truth that's missing from calculations, comps/analysis, and even that in-person visit. It finishes connecting the dots, so to speak.

Yet due diligence poses a substantial problem of its own. The problem is that being so thorough usually entails spending considerable time and money. So, in a way, you're making a major investment (your time and money) whether or not you ever make the explicit investment later to buy the property.

The whole thing can seem like a sort of catch-22. A case of "damned if you do, damned if you don't."

Yet there is a solution.

It can be expensive and byzantine. But it's a solution nevertheless, and we call it the closing process.

The closing process serves as the ultimate "safety net" at the end before entering a deal. It protects you from any hidden things you may have missed, externally. And it also protects you, perhaps surprisingly, from yourself.

On that latter point, the idea is that due diligence helps you slow down. You don't end up derailing your own deal as a result of being too eager to do it. This is a major pitfall that I routinely see among investors, particularly the newbies.

Usually these over-eager investors will err in one of two ways.

First, they won't negotiate enough time on purchase and sales agreements to conduct the proper due diligence before putting down their deposit ("going hard"). These newbies, and even experienced guys, don't allow themselves at least twenty days to handle the due diligence. They think that the process can be fast-tracked.

So instead of allotting twenty days or more (standard for a large commercial real estate property), they might try to do all the due diligence in say, a week. The investor's agreement with the seller (the purchase and sales agreement) would therefore reflect this. It would state that after that one week, the investor's deposit would become nonrefundable.

Do you think the investor in that case is going to be rushed? Under the gun, as they say? Absolutely.

And with such a short time frame for due diligence, such an investor is setting themselves up to fail. For what if they miss something? Something essential that a twenty day (or more) due diligence period would have brought to light.

Imagine missing a piece of the puzzle like that, only to find it later after your deposit has become nonrefundable.

Or, maybe you don't err like that. It's not the only way I see investors stumble. As I mentioned before, there's another side to this pitfall of being overly eager and rushing to do a deal. The closing process can save you from this second aspect of the pitfall. But you should still know what to look out for.

The other part of being overly eager and rushing is that you may bite off more than you can chew. Not literally. But in the sense of overestimating your ability to raise capital.

In such cases, you'd have unrealistic expectations on how much money you could raise, as a syndicator, for the down payment. Those expectations could be that you believed you could raise more money in total than you were actually capable of raising. Or you might be capable of raising such money, but not in the length of time you envisioned.

All this talk of "being realistic" isn't meant to discourage you. You can still "dream big" and adopt a 10X approach to life.

I, for one, will be the last one to ever advise playing "small ball" in life. If I'd settled and been more "realistic," I'd still be back in Australia at an abysmal 9-to-5 job.

But in my case, and in yours as well, it's important to recognize that there are definitely times to be realistic.

One such time would be, as noted, when you're assessing how much you can raise as a syndicator in a deal. That's a definite time to think realistically on whether, for example, you can raise $1 million in two months, as the down payment on a $4 million deal. Is your network of investors really at the level where you'd be able to raise the money in time?

If not, you might be better off going after a smaller property. Perhaps you'd look at one where the total investment was only $1 million. Then, in the same two-month period, you'd only needed to raise $250,000 initially as the standard 25% down payment.

Make sense?

And can you see as well, in a larger sense, how the closing process saves you? How it keeps you from overestimating yourself, rushing, and getting tripped up in all the other external and internal ways discussed thus far?

I think you get the idea now. This "closing process thing" is kind of important.

So let's get right into it.

What we'll cover now are the six basic stages of the closing process. These stages each follow one another in sequence.

Some aspects of them may vary slightly depending on where in the US your potential deal is located. This would be the case with title companies. In certain states, your lawyer, or a seller's lawyer, can act as the title company, helping to facilitate in closing the deal. In other states, though, the title company is a third-party vendor that facilitates the closing process. Here, you'd have both attorneys and a title company involved in the deal.

Even with differences like this, however, the basic closing process generally follows a six-stage sequence.

Without further ado, let's see what's involved with it.

STAGE 1 – SUBMITTING AN OFFER

The closing process begins as soon as you and the buyer come to an agreement after submitting your initial offer. This agreement is still somewhat tenuous, as it probably includes many contingencies, but you've both agreed to make a sale under some specific set of circumstances.

With the initial offer, you're submitting a Letter of Intent (LOI) to the seller. This letter makes a "soft," non-binding offer to the seller on their property.

Naturally, your offer names the property you wish to buy from the seller and the amount of money you're willing to pay for it. Along with those items, the offer also outlines the overall process and any contingencies that accompany your offer, and spells out everything that needs to happen during the first sixty days of closing, including a list of documents required to be submitted by the seller to you (the buyer) in order to conduct a full due diligence. This way you and the seller both have a clear sense of everything that's going to happen as you advance towards potentially doing the deal. The seller will know, for example, that you want to check out the plumbing and HVAC issues, get a building inspection, and pull a title report as part of the due diligence. They won't be surprised to learn that these were contingencies to you going ahead with the deal.

Speaking of surprises, it shouldn't come as a surprise to you that the

LOI is time-sensitive. It's usually good for a period of forty-eight to seventy-two hours after the seller receives it.

Also, so there's no confusion, let me point out that residential real estate deals usually don't have a LOI. In those cases (residential RE), the document you provide the seller will probably be a Residential Purchase Agreement. This agreement serves as a two-way contract between both parties. It's more binding than the LOI, which is used primarily in commercial real estate.

Since commercial RE is my primary focus, I've chosen to highlight the LOI here. Still, you should recognize the distinction and know about Residential Purchase Agreements.

In either case, the initial document (LOI or Residential Purchase Agreement) still lays out the basic elements of the transaction, describing, as we've said, the price, the due diligence you'll do, the time you have to complete the due diligence, and any additional time needed to organize financing for the property.

In addition, the initial document for your offer specifies who pays for what along the way. That should come as good news to you, since it means that you alone may not have to shoulder the full financial "weight" of the closing process. How much you pay versus how much the seller pays will all be stated in the initial offer document.

Given everything this document covers, you can think of it as the road map and the rule book for the transaction. And for the document to have any real power, you shouldn't rush putting it together. Take the time, whether you do it yourself or with help, to carefully craft your LOI or Residential Purchase Agreement document. Make sure it's clear and spells out all the responsibilities of each party along the way and everything else that's expected.

To help you do that, I've provided an example of the LOI I use.

Again, I'm mainly focused on real estate's commercial side, so this is the document I can best address here. You'll see it on the next two pages.

> **Example Letter - Omitted by Google Docs, but visible in Word Version of Chapter**
>
> download the sample LOI at
> www.reedgoossens.com/LOI-sample

For the LOI above, all of the sensitive information (i.e., names, companies, etc.) has justifiably been omitted. Even with the omissions, you can still get a sense of what a standard LOI consists of.

Make sure, though, that you do more than merely cut and paste my example, and then think you're done with the LOI. I've given you a good starting point, but you still need to put some thought into all this.

You also need to think about the other things you're submitting to the seller. You can't just send an LOI alone. You must submit financials with it. Financials prove to the seller that you have enough financial backing to buy the property. That you're in good shape, essentially.

What do I mean by "financials"?

This usually consists of two documents, one or both of which you'll send along with your LOI.

1. A POF ("Proof of Funds") – The POF dictates the equity you'll be bringing to the table as down payment for a property. It's normally between 20% and 30% of the offer price.

2. A loan pre-approval letter – You'd send this letter along with the POF, if you're using debt to purchase the property. The pre-approval letter is a letter from your financial institution stating

that they have pre-approved you for a given loan amount.

As a tip here, let me advise you to also send the seller records from any other similar-sized transactions you've done in the past. Doing so further illustrates to the seller and their broker that you're competent and can execute on deals.

Nonetheless, documents showing past experience are not a requirement. So if you're reading this and have limited experience, just submit the basic documents (LOI, POF, and potentially the pre-approval letter) to the seller, but also find a partner who does have experience in order to show credibility. (Refer to the establishing your A-Team chapter regarding building credibility.)

Another aspect of making your offer that needs to be addressed is the closing period. I've alluded to it at various points up to now, saying that you should give yourself enough time.

Seriously, though, how much time is enough time?

And, more generally speaking, how long is this closing period supposed to last?

Let's get clear on both of those questions now, so you have accurate knowledge of the closing period.

The Closing Period

When we speak of the closing period, in commercial real estate, we're typically looking at a total of sixty days. At a minimum.

In that time, the first twenty to thirty days will be due diligence. We've belabored the point already, but please, once more—give yourself enough time on this. Don't make the newbie mistake of not stipulating a long enough due diligence period.

In addition to the due diligence period, there will then be fifteen to thirty days for financing. This matters, of course, so that money can actually change hands in the transaction.

In order to do due diligence and review financing, you'll need four important documents from the seller within the first week of due diligence.

These documents probably aren't the only ones the seller will be sending you. But they are, without a doubt, the most important in helping you obtain debt financing on your deal. Your bank will want to see these as early as possible.

The four documents you need are:

1. The Profit & Loss Statement – showing the seller's profits and losses in the last two years of operations.

2. The Rent Roll – a summary of all renters and what they pay, along with their deposit.

3. Any contracts or statements displaying additional income the building might be generating, beyond rental income. Examples here would include laundry and cable costs.

4. Tax statements for the past two years.

With these four basic documents from the seller, you can get 90% confident on the deal. You'll then be able to get the last 10% of the way to full confidence after you've completed the full due diligence process.

Depending on the particular deal, you may also get an offer memorandum from the seller. If so, their broker will likely pull this document together and give it to you.

With the offer memorandum and the other documents, you can

proceed through the closing period we've described, which for commercial real estate is going to be a minimum of sixty days.

If you're dealing with residential properties, then the length will be shorter. Those in a residential property deal are typically looking at a thirty-day closing process. In that case, there's usually a ten-day inspection period, followed by a one- to two-week financing period, totaling thirty days for the deal to be reviewed and then close.

Ok, now for the fun part.

Let's say you make an offer to the seller, submitting a LOI in Stage 1 of the closing process. Suppose the seller then approves your offer, signing the LOI.

You're now ready to officially start on Stage 2 of the closing process. This is where your offer has been accepted and you do the *deeper* due diligence I've made so many mentions of.

STAGE 2 – OFFER ACCEPTED

With this next stage, money has now officially entered into the dynamic. You've deposited what we call "earnest money" into an escrow account.

The escrow account will be managed by the title company. That company acts as a neutral third party in the transaction. Sort of a referee or enforcer, if you will, to make sure you and the seller are both playing fair on finances and never deviate from whatever ground rules you set up front.

The earnest money is essentially an "are you serious?" deposit. It shows the seller that you're not just window shopping and are actually serious about doing this deal.

The seller responds to your offer by giving the escrow the ability to transfer ownership of their property. This means that if the deal goes through, the escrow can then formally make you the property's owner.

As the seller and you the buyer take these two steps, you become locked into escrow together.

I say "locked" yet at this stage you can still get your money out. If the deal doesn't hold up once you start scratching the surface, you're not screwed. There's still hope, provided you have good contingency in your offer. The right contingency lets you back out with minimal, if any, damage to your wallet.

An example of a contingency you might put in your offer would be a loan contingency that says the offer is contingent on you obtaining the right bank financing for the property. Perhaps you want to get financing at 5.5% over ten years, four years interest-only, and amortized across thirty years.

These kinds of terms could make sense if you're nervous you won't qualify for the financing from your bank. Having such terms in the offer allows you to back out of the deal. It's your "safety net," though it does tend to be frowned on and conveys definite "newbie" status.

Another example of a contingency you'd put in your offer involves the four documents you're requesting from the seller. Your offer would stipulate with this contingency that due diligence wouldn't start until the seller sends you the four initial documents you've asked for.

Once you've gotten those four documents, you can begin to dig and investigate the deal on a deeper level, proceeding now into the full due-diligence process.

To do that, you now request a more in-depth collection of paperwork from the seller that lets you really know what you're in for with this potential deal.

Here's what you specifically request at this next stage, Stage 2:

- Copies of all leases
- The most recent financial statements
- Any tenant credit reports
- A leasing status report from the broker (pending any rental applications)
- Leases of subsidies tenants (if any) – These are people who are on government rental income and are using that to pay rent at the property. Section 8ers, in other words.
- A delinquency report (historical) – This report shows who's been delinquent on their rent and how often. For example, in the last twelve months, has anyone been behind two months in paying the rent?
- Operating statements – From the previous two years
- A certified rent roll, which includes security deposits
- A schedule of all CAPEX within the past two years
- All service contracts (pest control, snow removal, etc.)
- As-built surveys of the property – These are the plans of the property, how it was built, and any other relevant architectural and structural documents
- Copies of any liens or insurance claims within the past five years
- A lead-based paint disclosure
- Copies of utilities invoices

Getting these documents enables you to go back to your initial analysis and verify your assumptions. You can now see how right—or how wrong—you've been about: existing rents, vacancies, utilities costs, and expenses ratios.

In the best case, you'll be right and everything you thought is on track.

You're *not* done yet, however.

It's time now to call in the pros...

STAGE 3 – LOOKING IT OVER

When you "call in the pros," you're seeking the advice of outside experts. Such experts have specialized knowledge in the various areas that need to be considered as you look over a property, prior to closing on it.

Seeking professional help makes sense because you can only tell so much about a property on your own. And by this point in the closing process, you'll have reviewed the property to the best of your abilities. Qualified experts can therefore help you bridge the gap between your knowledge and a complete picture of the property.

In terms of specific experts, you'll be working with a few different ones, both at the property ("on-site") and away from it ("off-site").

On the property, you'll collaborate with a general inspector. They'll check all of the building's systems to make sure everything's in good shape and code compliant. Given the "general" in their name, a general inspector may recommend that you bring in further specialists.

Other specialists could give you guidance in any of the following areas: pest problems, foundation problems, electrical problems, plumbing problems, structural problems, safety problems, roofing problems, and code problems.

Each of those areas is definitely worth checking out. It's the only way to really know the condition of what you're buying.

Still, don't get the wrong idea here on hiring experts. Chances are you probably won't need to hire one for every single aspect of checking out a property. But if you do find a reason to be concerned on one particular area—say, plumbing—it's well worth investigating.

In addition, since your property will be in the US, you'll need to be aware of lead paint and asbestos issues. Those two dangerous materials are often found in US buildings. To ensure the safety of yourself and your tenants, make sure you investigate whether either material has been used in or around your prospective property.

Also, look beyond your own property and review the local history to get a broader sense of whether lead paint and asbestos have been used in the states and cities where you're planning to invest.

Finally, if you're planning on building, you may want to bring in engineers and architects to inspect the site. Find out if the soil on the site can support what you've planned. This will ensure you don't have a "sinking feeling" later, as you watch your construction literally sink into the ground.

STAGE 4 – HITTING THE BOOKS

Even if you're not going to build anything, you'll still want to understand the "lay of the land." This means becoming knowledge-able on what the environment around a prospective property is like.

I always recommend obtaining a Phase I environmental report from the seller. If the seller doesn't have a Phase I report, you will need to get one developed. This report is a historical study of the local area around your property, which will determine if any environmental issues are present near your site. For example, a neighboring property might have been a gas station back in the day; there might be cause for concern as gas stations have underground fuel storage tanks and these tanks might have degraded over time and potentially leaked into the ground water table and surrounding soils, which may have contaminated the soils on your site. If a Phase 1 report comes back stating there are potential environmental issues, I would recommend walking away from the deal. Dealing with contaminated soils is better left to the seasoned investors who know how to deal with the issues and the cost impact on the overall investment. A Phase 1 report costs between $1,500 and $5,000, depending on the size of property. It is a small price to pay in order to avoid environmental issues.

Another useful report at this stage would be a Preliminary Title Report, sometimes called a prelim. A title company can provide you with this document.

If you're reading this as a foreign investor, a prelim is something to pay particular attention to. That's because it's a peculiarity of the US real estate system and may be different in your home country.

A prelim is necessary because unlike many countries, the US doesn't have a government land registration system. There's no government agency in America that tracks ownership of each parcel of land and lays out ownership and other land rights.

Rather, the US takes a more hands-off approach, relying on what's called a recording system. Under this system, anyone making a real estate transaction is encouraged to record the transaction with the government agency. The encouragement's there, but the government itself doesn't do any sort of review. Instead, it simply records the documents provided.

As a result, at the time of the sale, the government doesn't actually check that the seller has the power to sell the land. Nor is there any checking to confirm that the seller really owns the land in the first place.

To fill this void, title companies have stepped in. They provide a report on the ownership of the land (i.e., the prelim). A prelim details not only ownership but also any defects in the title to the land. Such defects would include outstanding loans or liens taken out against the land by the current owner.

Title companies further support you by offering insurance against other title issues that they may have missed. In this way, they essentially offer a guarantee that their prelim report is accurate, so you can be confident that you're really buying what you think you're buying, that the seller really can sell it, and that you'll be protected if unpleasant surprises should occur down the line.

To wrap up this stage (Stage 4) of the closing process, here's the complete list of property inspection items. These are among the primary things you'll want to get inspected by a certified third party:

- HVAC system
- Plumbing
- Asbestos
- Roof
- Structural issues
- Contaminated soils – Ask the seller for a Phase I report. If they don't have one, get a third party to complete this report for you.

STAGE 5 – LOCKING IT IN ("GOING HARD")

Ok, at this stage, you're nearly there.

Seriously, I mean it this time.

You really are in the final, final "homestretch" of the closing process.

This is the point after due diligence is completed and it's almost time to wrap up the deal.

Right now, you may go back and renegotiate the purchase price with the seller if there are major deferred maintenance issues (HVAC system, roof) or any other issues like liens on the property.

On the other hand, if nothing needs to be renegotiated and everyone is in agreement, it's time to "go hard" with your money.

This is the point when the earnest money you placed in escrow becomes nonrefundable. Since it's nonrefundable, you'll lose the earnest money if you walk away from the deal between now and closing day.

STAGE 6 – GETTING IT FUNDED

Rounding out this final stretch in the closing process comes financing. If you're using financing to purchase a property, you won't be the only party who has to sign off. The lender will need to review the deal to make sure that the building in it is a suitable security for their loan (aka the financing period).

The lender will verify this by doing their own appraisal of the building's worth. If they appraise it at a lower value than the money you've offered for the deal, the lender won't provide the mortgage for the full amount that you expected. You'll have to either make up the difference yourself or open up talks again with the seller.

MAKING A DECISION

Once your financing is set, it's time to make a decision.

Right now, after everything you've seen in the closing process, are you going to go through with this deal?

Forget about the earnest money for a moment.

Forget, as well, about your own eagerness to do the deal.

Look solely at all that you know at this juncture in time. All that's been revealed to you through each of the preceding stages.

Do you want to proceed with this deal or not?

If you do want to proceed, you can continue on with the deal and see it through.

If not, you can renegotiate with the seller.

Or you can simply walk away.

Each of these options is yours to take, depending on what you wish to do. The options and their full ramifications will have been spelled out in advance in your written agreement with the seller. (*This is, by the way, why a well-crafted agreement is so important.)

So, do you proceed, renegotiate, or walk?

I can't answer that for you. Nor should I. (Imagine all the potential lawsuits!)

What I can tell you, though, is that there are no guarantees in life.

That's not to say you should or shouldn't do a particular deal. It's simply recognizing that any investment decision carries financial, legal, and physical risks with it.

It's really no different than my decision to "level up" to a new life on my terms in America. You know how badly my knee was shaking then, as I sat with my girlfriend at the airport in Sydney, right before we caught the plane to New York. My shaking knee reflected my own awareness of the fact that a substantial investment—regardless of what it is—will have risks. It comes with the territory, whether we're talking about my story or your own, as a real estate investor closing on a deal.

Your story in a given deal may or may not have a happy ending. As the hero in that story, you can valiantly perform all the investigations we've described, every last one of them, without ever getting truly definitive answers.

You may never learn, for example, whether the plumbing at a prospective property will break. Or whether the earth around the property is going to split open. The likelihood of such scenarios may remain unknown to you until they happen.

Is this then grounds for you to walk from a deal?

Maybe. But then maybe not.

You have to decide that, knowing what I've said on risk. And taking comfort too in the knowledge that by this point in the closing process, you've gathered all the information you possibly can, considered all the probabilities, and evaluated all the risks. If you've truly done that— not shortcutting or bypassing any of the less-appealing parts—then whatever decision you make will likely be correct because you are knowledgeable about all the issues involved with investing here in the US after reading this book. And knowledge is power, but knowledge combined with action leads to ultimate success.

CLOSING

Let's say you decide to proceed with the deal. You've done all your due diligence and investigations. You've satisfied yourself on any issues that you've found. You've potentially renegotiated with the seller. And now you're ready to close.

Assuming the bank is OK with the terms and conditions you've arranged earlier, they'll now fund escrow.

Once the escrow's been funded, the escrow company makes the change in the deed, handing out money and title to the appropriate parties.

The closing process, with its seemingly infinite number of parts and details, is now over. Like really, truly over.

Well, except for that one part.

Where you now go and...

No, I'm joking. Seriously kidding. That's the end of the closing process. There's nothing else now, just you, your property, and a whole lot of fun as you embark on making your new investment property work for you.

How exactly do you make it work for you?

We've spoken at length on that in many of the earlier chapters. But there's a unique way we have yet to really dig into. It's kind of like the "best-kept secret" in REI. Those of us who are actually doing it and are in the game know this and love it. Yet it's still a secret to many of the REI "window shoppers," those who are on the outside looking in, excited by the supposed profits of real estate but unwilling to enter and find out what's in store for them (no pun intended!).

In the next section, another of our shorter "mini chapters," we'll be covering what this "best-kept secret" is. I think you'll like what you find, so join me now in the next section.

COMFORT CHALLENGE

For this chapter, there's no comfort challenge. Frankly, it would be redundant, since the entire chapter is really about getting out of your comfort zone and putting a deal that you think is a "cracker" to the test. Testing to the fullest your assumptions on the deal, and then potentially stepping out of your comfort zone to do the deal.

Having already emphasized investigating and working hard to know everything about a prospective deal, there's no need for me to give your further homework. Take this chapter off. Save your strength for the closing process on your first deal. Trust me, you'll need it!

★★ AUSSIE-ISMS ★★

In the same spirit of saving your strength, I'm also not going to bombard you with tons of Aussie slang in this chapter either. Here are some softball bits of slang for you to have a look at:

1. "Don't cut your nose off to spite your face" – Don't react in anger in a way that hurts you more than others

2. "Don't be a flaming idiot" – A really dumb person (Do I really need to translate this one for you?)

CHAPTER 11

RINSE AND REPEAT

The "best-kept secret in REI." Remember that? I promised to tell you all about it in this chapter. In keeping with that promise, let's talk now about this supposed "secret."

The "secret" to which I'm referring is the 1031 exchange. It's a method by which real estate investors can soften the "pain" of having to pay taxes.

Let me be clear from the onset that I'm *not* a tax specialist. Nor am I an attorney. Hopefully, you already realize this after hearing similar disclaimers in our preceding chapters. But if not, now you know.

Anyway, for the 1031 exchange, it's going to make taxes more bearable for us as real estate investors. How exactly?

Through deferment and reinvestment.

Those are the keys, according to my good friend, attorney William Exeter of Exeter 1031 Exchange Services. He's been helping investors do 1031 exchanges for over 30 years, so it's safe to call him an expert.

Exeter defines the 1031 exchange as a process by which an investor can sell their investment property and defer the payment of capital gains taxes on it. Rather than paying those taxes immediately, an investor is able to "roll" them over into another "like-kind" investment property that they acquire. The "rollover" happens once the investor has sold the original asset.

As a basic example, say you've purchased a $400,000 property. Over the time you have owned it, the value increases to $500,000. You then decide to sell it, but don't want to be hit with capital gains taxes. You might therefore elect to do a 1031 exchange.

Here are some basic rules:

1. Upon the sale of your first asset, you have up to 45 days from the date of sale to identify potential replacement properties to be purchased with your sales proceeds.

2. Once you've identified a potential replacement property, you have 180 days from the sales date of your original asset to complete the transaction.

3. The new asset must be of "like-kind," which means if you sold a real estate asset you must buy another real estate asset. This third limitation keeps you, for example, from selling a piece of artwork and using the proceeds to buy a piece of real estate. Artwork for real estate is not a "like-kind exchange." Instead a "like-kind exchange" means you can exchange property used in your trade or business or held for investment for property to be used in the same way.

Along with those basic rules, there are also three criteria for identifying a replacement asset. The replacement asset will be what you acquire and "roll" your capital gains taxes into.

The criteria for identifying new real estate assets in a 1031 exchange are:

- **The three-property criteria**: You may identify up to three different properties as potential purchases within the 45-day identification period and regardless of the total fair market value of the properties.

- **The 200% criteria**: Alternatively, you can identify an unlimited number of replacement properties, as long as the total fair market value of all properties does not exceed 200% of the value of all relinquished property in the same exchange.

- **The 95% criteria**: Another alternative is you may identify alternative properties, as long as you receive at least 95% percent of the value of all identified replacement properties before the end of the exchange period.

· · · · · · · · · ·

I realize that these rules and criteria may sound detailed and perhaps confusing too. Yet you probably get the overall idea and realize that 1031 exchanges can be absolute lifesavers, where taxes are concerned.

If that's the case, you're likely intrigued at this point by the idea of a 1031 exchange and using it to defer taxes. I know I certainly was, when hearing about it for the first time a few years back. There's nothing comparable to it where I'm from, back in Australia. I'd imagine as well that if you're outside the US, your country probably doesn't have anything like the 1031 exchange either. Perhaps this is why it's such a "secret." Who knows, really? But now you know about it and you can potentially employ the 1031 exchange in your REI efforts.

Let's say you decide to complete a 1031 exchange. Here's an in-depth example of what you could expect.

For our example now, suppose you're going to do a transaction involving a property that will produce $100,000 in capital gains. If you do a 1031 exchange, the $100K will then be rolled into another "like-kind" property that you acquire.

Let's say the property is a single-family house. You originally bought this house and paid $400,000 for it. Since then, the house has appreciated as an asset and is now worth $500,000. This means you've made $100,000 in profit (from $500,000 minus $400,000).

To access your profits, you're now planning to sell the house. At the same time, however, you're keenly aware that selling the house is a transaction and will therefore be subject to federal and state taxes.

Those taxes stand to "eat" approximately a third of the $100K, taking approximately $33,333 and leaving you with approximately $66,667.

Yikes! That's a scary thought. And not just because of the "666" part (supposedly that's the devil's number). No, it's downright terrifying to think of only being left with 2/3 of your returns on an investment.

Fortunately, however, you don't have to accept that. You can proceed with the 1031 exchange, as we've said, and roll that $100K in full towards the acquisition of your next property.

The trade-off here is that you're not pocketing the $100K directly. So it's *not* going into your bank account to pay for say, a vacation, a new car, your kid's college tuition, and more. No, the money is instead being used for your next investment, helping you expand your portfolio and scale up in larger deals.

That's the "exchange" part of a 1031 exchange. You're exchanging one investment property—with its profits and taxes—for another one.

With the second property, you may cash-out and pay your capital gains taxes. But then maybe you don't. Maybe you choose instead to do the 1031 exchange again, a second time, rolling the profit from property number two into a third investment property.

At that point, you'd seemingly have to settle down, right? I mean, this 1031 exchange stuff probably has a cap on it. Some kind of a limit. Like you're limited to only ever doing a 1031 exchange two times. And then once you go for the third time, you'll be in violation of the law.

Nope. There are no such limits on the 1031 exchange. None that I know of. And none that your tax lawyer—whom you should consult—will likely be able to spot.

Limits really don't exist for the 1031 exchange. You can do it, and do it, and do it, and do it, and...You get the idea.

Just don't fall in love with 1031 exchanges. Not now. Nor at any point in your time as an investor. The reason is that a 1031 exchange isn't always the best course of action. There may be times when you actually should recognize the taxes now, as opposed to deferring them.

Look, I know that may sound crazy. But it's what Exeter told me directly. When I had him on my podcast (*Investing in the US*), he was emphatic that the 1031 exchange is not always the right course of action.

How then do you know if it makes sense?

According to Exeter, there are two things you can do. First, think about the transaction as an investor. Move your thoughts of tax consequences onto the "back burner" for just a moment and reflect on all that's involved in the transaction you're considering.

As you do that, ask yourself whether this will be a wise business decision. Consider, too, whether it's the right investment decision for you, specifically, as an investor.

If you can answer both of those questions with a firm "Yes," then it's time to think about taxes. You can take your thoughts of tax consequences off the "back burner" to consider at last, how taxes might "burn" you and whether a 1031 exchange would make sense.

As you mull that over, don't do so alone. Instead, sit down with your tax advisor and get their input. Leverage their expertise to get a complete sense of your exposure and whether it's appropriate for you to defer taxes or recognize them now.

Another point on the 1031 exchange is it involves "deferring" taxes.

Notice how I'm using that word "defer," rather than say "escape" or "slide out of"?

I'm using "defer" specifically because you're *not* evading your taxes and just flat out not paying them. That's called tax evasion and it's illegal.

So no, you're *not* going to evade taxes. Instead, the idea is that you can defer them, paying taxes at a later date, as opposed to right now.

As long as we're talking about the law, let's be clear too, that 1031 exchanges are perfectly legal. There are no loopholes or "grey areas" of the law either.

No, the 1031 exchange is so legal that it's actually written into the IRS tax code. This means then that if you read through the code, and can stay awake amidst all the boring details, you'll see a section devoted to 1031s.

The section on 1031 exchanges isn't exactly new either. Not unless your definition of "new" is anything from 1921 onward.

1921? Yeah, that's the year when 1031 exchanges first appeared in the US tax code. So they've been around for nearly a century.

The bottom line then is that you're fully justified in doing a 1031 exchange and deferring taxes. The question, though, is whether you should. Is it the right decision for you personally?

While we're on you and your personal decisions, I want to discuss a larger concept that's related to the 1031 exchange and expands our discussion in a new and highly exciting direction.

I call it a "concept," but it's more like a philosophy. A philosophy that I strongly encourage you to embrace and stay mindful of, throughout your REI journey.

It's the philosophy of "rinse and repeat." The idea that you're not just buying a single investment property and leaving it at that. I mean, you could. There's nothing stopping you. But I don't recommend it. What I recommend, as do my mentors and countless other top investors, is that you "rinse and repeat."

To "rinse and repeat" means that you invest in real estate with the understanding that most of the steps you take are going to be repeated over and over again. You'll be buying a property, growing it as an investment, and then moving on to the next one.

As you do, perhaps you'll use a 1031 exchange. Or you might decide instead to pay the taxes right then. But either way you'll still continue on to your next investment property.

And the property after that.

And the property after that.

Continuing until you decide to stop, as you have reached your financial goals. If that day ever comes. Which is really anyone's guess at this point.

No need for us to speculate on it now. The idea is only that you're going to be at this for a while, doing the same steps over and over.

Thinking about it now, especially with the idea of repeating steps, I see REI and "rinse and repeat" as comparable to dancing. In this case, the property would be your dance partner, whom you lead through the steps. Then, as it makes sense, you trade dance partners and do it over again.

All the while, the music is dictating how you dance. This makes the music akin to the individual real estate market you're in. A fast-moving piece of music will therefore make you dance differently than will music at a slower pace.

The music is always changing too, so you'll need to continually adjust to the changing tempos, both while dancing (in the analogy) and while investing in real estate.

It's going to be fun, though. At least I think so. And you'll probably agree. Chances are you'll come to enjoy cycling through the REI process, "rinsing and repeating" your way to rivers of passive income. Passive income that flows to you so strongly that it can never be dammed (in the river sense) by a damn(!) 9-to-5 job.

Financial freedom, in other words. That's where we're headed. Or rather, it's where you're headed. Provided, of course, that you do enter REI, that you take all we've covered here and then take action on your own accord.

Will you?

Don't answer that. Not yet. For at this point, it would be too easy to just nod your head along and say "Yes," drunk perhaps on all this talk from the book.

I'd rather you sober up and think, really think, about everything in this book. Think about how it translates into your own life. Your own day-to-day efforts.

Are you, for example, sitting in your *prison cell*— sorry, I meant your office.

Are you sitting in your *office*, as I was in the first chapter, feeling disappointed? Feeling as though you've hit a kind of ceiling on where you can go. Give that some serious consideration. Are you sick of exchanging your time for money?

Think too about the steps you'll take to get started in REI. We've covered those steps in this book. If you'll recall, the process was essentially to educate yourself while meeting other investors, raising the necessary capital, and building your REI team. Then, when it makes sense, you proceed to do your first deal, following that deal, as we've just said, with another and another and so on.

Think about all of this.

Now, add your life goals to the mix. What's your life's true purpose? What is it, as well, that will give your life a sense of meaning and direction? Time freedom?

Make sure you answer these questions on life goals. They may seem cheesy, yet these questions are just as important as any of the others. For with REI you'll finally have the freedom to follow whatever you deem to be your life's true purpose.

If your purpose is volunteering, you'll finally have the freedom to do so.

Perhaps you'll choose to do something close to home, helping out at a local food bank or at any of a bazillion other charities, making a contribution that way and letting such a contribution be your life's purpose.

Of course, you might not go in a philanthropic direction. You could use REI, instead, to support your "charity mission" of feeding yourself the best in French cheeses, Russian caviar, and Greek baklava, since you're currently "starving" to experience the wonders of different cultures around the world.

If that were your "mission," well...there's nothing inherently wrong with it. Nor is there anything wrong with using REI to fulfill your "life's purpose" of owning luxury cars and living on the beach somewhere.

Far be it for me to judge you on any of that. If it's what you want to do, then REI can help you to do so.

Understand, however, that it's going to take time and hard work. You will *not* get rich overnight from investing in real estate. It just doesn't happen, and I'd be doing you a tremendous disservice in making such a claim.

This is not to say that you can't ever enjoy the kind of luxuries described here. With enough time and with enough hard work, you may eventually have that option as a real estate investor.

Nonetheless, you'll only have such an option if you take action. And that's a choice.

It may be a difficult or even frightening choice to make. Yet it's nonetheless a choice you'll have to make.

The good news, however, is that you're not alone. In making your choice of whether to enter REI, you're following in the footsteps of countless other RE investors.

I would be one of them, and you've read in this book how I made the decision. How, in my case, it frightened me so much that my leg shook when I boarded that flight to leave my life in Australia on a journey to achieve my goals in the US.

Yet I made the decision and I chose to pursue REI, making a serious commitment to it.

What's the difference between me and you? What is it that separates us in our respective abilities to succeed at REI?

It's not our family backgrounds. Remember how I said both my parents worked average-paying jobs and we lived a middle-class life? So it's not like I waltzed into REI with a million dollars in "free money."

It's not connections either. I had none in Australia or in the US, as I was getting started.

Actually, the odds were even more against me since I didn't have a job in the US when I first moved there. No job, nor any connections, and an initial six-month limit on how long I could legally be in the country.

Talk about an uphill battle. It was really, if you think about it, completely insane. Moving to the other side of the world with no job, no connections, and no residency, to try your hand at a profession you have *zero* experience in.

Yet I made it work. And if I can do that, what's stopping you? Especially if you're already living in the US and have a true "home-court advantage."

But even if you're not in the US and live abroad, what's truly stopping you from entering US real estate as an investor? That may entail moving here. Or you may continue living abroad. Regardless, though, you can still get started.

I'm proof of that. Let my example serve then as a continual reminder to you.

A reminder of how doable this is. All of it.

A reminder, too, of how you can truly take life into your own hands and reshape it to match whatever your vision is.

Whether you do that, though, is—as you're probably sick of hearing by now—a choice. A decision for you and you alone to make.

If I can help you on that, in any way, feel free to reach out through my website (www.ReedGoossens.com).

Oh, and in case you haven't realized by now, we've come to the end of this book. Sad as it may be, there aren't any more chapters left. Well, chapters in the sense of this book.

The next chapter in your own life, though, may be just around the corner. Depending on what you decide, after reading this book, you may soon embark on your next chapter in life as a real estate investor.

Wherever the road ahead leads, I want to thank you for taking time to read through my book. As an author, I'm grateful that you read my book up to the end here. It's the highest compliment any author can receive, so thanks for that.

Best of luck as well in your REI efforts, if that's where your road leads. And should that indeed be the case, then, quite simply...

Remember, be bold, be brave and go out and give life a crack!!

Happy investing!

APPENDIX A

U.S. FEDERAL TAX ON PERSONAL INCOME - 2018

Single

Taxable Income	Tax Rate
$0 - $9,525	10% of taxable income
$9,526 - $38,700	$952.50 *plus* 12% of the amount over $9,525
$38,701 - $82,500	$4,453.50 *plus* 22% of the amount over $38,700
$82,501 - $157,500	$14,089.50 *plus* 24% of the amount over $82,500
$157,501 - $200,000	$32,089.50 *plus* 32% of the amount over $157,500
$200,001 - $500,000	$45,689.50 *plus* 35% of the amount over $200,000
$500,001 or more	$150,689.50 *plus* 37% of the amount over $500,000

Married Filing Jointly or Qualifying Widow(er)

Taxable Income	Tax Rate
$0 - $19,050	10% of taxable income
$19,051 - $77,400	$1,905 *plus* 12% of the amount over $19,050
$77,401 - $165,000	$8,907 *plus* 22% of the amount over $77,400
$165,001 - $315,000	$28,179 *plus* 24% of the amount over $165,000
$315,001 - $400,000	$64,179 *plus* 32% of the amount over $315,000
$400,001 - $600,000	$91,379 *plus* 35% of the amount over $400,000
$600,001 or more	$161,379 *plus* 37% of the amount over $600,000

Married Filing Separately

Taxable Income	Tax Rate
$0 - $9,525	10% of taxable income
$9,526 - $38,700	$952.50 *plus* 12% of the amount over $9,525
$38,701 - $82,500	$4,453.50 *plus* 22% of the amount over $38,700
$82,501 - $157,500	$14,089.50 *plus* 24% of the amount over $82,500
$157,501 - $200,000	$32,089.50 *plus* 32% of the amount over $157,500
$200,001 - $300,000	$45,689.50 *plus* 35% of the amount over $200,000
$300,001 or more	$80,689.50 *plus* 37% of the amount over $300,000

Head of Household

Taxable Income	Tax Rate
$0 - $13,600	10% of taxable income
$13,601 - $51,800	$1,360 *plus* 12% of the amount over $13,600
$51,801 - $82,500	$5,944 *plus* 22% of the amount over $51,800
$82,501 - $157,500	$12,698 *plus* 24% of the amount over $82,500
$157,501 - $200,000	$30,698 *plus* 32% of the amount over $157,500
$200,001 - $500,000	$44,298 *plus* 35% of the amount over $200,000
$500,001 or more	$149,298 *plus* 37% of the amount over $500,000

www.irs.com/articles/2018-federal-tax-rates-personal-exemptions-and-standard-deductions

APPENDIX B

U.S. INVESTING ABBREVIATIONS

AMORT – Amortization

APR – Annual Percentage Rate

ARM – Adjustable Rate Mortgage

ARV – After-Repaired Value

CAP – Capitalization (or Cap Rate)

CCIM – Certified Commercial Investment Member

CCR – Conditions, Covenants, and Restrictions

CFD – Contract for Deed

CLTV – Combined Loan-to-Value

CMA – Comparative Market Analysis

COCR or CCR – Cash-on-Cash Return

COF – Cost of Funds

COO or C of O – Certificate of Occupancy

CRE – Creative Real Estate

CRE – Commercial Real Estate

DBA – Doing Business As

DOS – Due on Sale Clause

DOT – Deed of Trust

DSCR or DCR or DSR – Debt Service Coverage Ratio

EMC – Earnest money contract

FCRA – Fair Credit Reporting Act

FDIC – Federal Deposit Insurance Corporation

FEMA – Federal Emergency Management Agency

FHA – Federal Housing Administration

FHLMC – Freddie Mac (Federal Home Loan Mortgage Corporation)

FMR – Fair Market Rent

FMV – Fair Market Value

FSBO – For Sale by Owner

GRM – Gross Rent Multiplier

HML – Hard Money Lender

HOA – Homeowners Association

HUD – Housing and Urban Development

I/O– Interest-Only (loan)

IRA – Individual Retirement Account

IRR – Internal Rate of Return

JV – Joint Venture

L/O – Lease Option

LLC – Limited Liability Company

LLP – Limited Liability Partnership

LtL – Loss to Lease

LOC – Line of Credit

LOI – Letter of Intent

LPOA – Limited Power of Attorney

LTV – Loan-to-Value

MAO – Maximum Allowable Offer

MLS – Multiple Listing Service

NNN – Triple Net Lease

NOI – Net Operating Income

NOO – Non-Owner Occupied

O/F – Owner Finance

OO – Owner Occupied

P&S – Purchase and Sale

PCF – Price to Cash Flow (ratio)

PITI – Principal, Interest, Taxes, and Insurance

POF – Proof of Funds

PUD – Planned Unit Development

REI – Real Estate Investing

REIA – Real Estate Investors Association

REO – Real Estate Owned

ROI – Return on Investment

RTO – Rent to Own

SFH – Single-Family House

SFR – Single-Family Residence

VA – Department of Veterans Affairs / Veterans Administration

REAL ESTATE LISTING ABBREVIATIONS

1C, 2C – 1 or 2 car Garage

2/1 – 2 bedrooms / 1 bathrooms

4/3 – 4 bedrooms / 3 bathrooms

3/4 Bath – toilet + sink + shower or tub

4/3/2 – 4 bedroom / 3 bath / 2 car garage

A/G PL – Above-Ground Pool

A/C – Air Conditioning

AC – Acre

Actv – Active

ALM – Aluminum Siding

APT – Apartment

ASB – Asbestos Siding

ASM – Assumptions

ATFN – Attic Fan

ATT – Attached Garage

BA – Bath

BALC – Balcony

BB – Baseboard Heat

BCH – Beach

BD – Bedroom

BKPORCH – Back Porch

BKYD – Backyard

BLDRS REDO – Builder's Renovation

BLT – Built-in

BOT – Boat Slip
BR – Bedroom
Brk – Brick
Brkf – Breakfast Area
Bsmt – Basement
Bulk – Bulkhead
Bung – Bungalow
C-fan – Ceiling Fan
CAC – Central Air Conditioning
Cbl,Cblh – Cable/Hookup
CCR – Conditions, Covenants, and Restrictions
Cdrcl – Cedar Closet
Cen – Central Air
Cent HVAC – Central Heat&Air
Cer – Ceramic Tile
CFan – Ceiling Fan
Chn – Chain Link Fence
Clap – Clapboard Siding
Clbhs – Clubhouse
Cldsc – Cul-de-sac
Clus – Cluster
Cnl – Canal
Col – Colonial
Cont – Contemporary
CPT – Carpet or Carport
Crk – Creek
Crprt – Carport
Crwl – Crawl Space
Cth – Cathedral Ceiling
CVAC – Central Vacuum
Cvga – Converted Garage
D/W – Dishwasher

Dbl– Double

Deco – Decorative Fence

DEDRS – Deed Restrictions

Det – Detached Garage

DhkpP – Dryer Hookup

Dk – Deck

DLM – Seller Disclaimer

DLO – Seller Disclosure

Dr -Dining Room

Dry – Clothes Dryer

Dsp – Garbage Disposal

DWF, DWAC – Deep Water/Access

EA – Exclusive Agency

EIK – Eat-in kitchen

ELE – Electric

ELV – Elevator

END – End Unit

ERS – Exclusive Right to Sell

Exr – Exercise Room

F/A Ht, FAH – Forced Air Heat

F-bmt – Finished Basement

Farm – Farmhouse

FRBO – For Rent By Owner

FDR – Formal Dining Room

FFBR – First Floor Bedroom

FFE – Furniture, Fixture, And Equipment

Fha – Forced Hot Air

FHA – Federal Housing Administration

FLR – Floor Furnace

FIN LL – Finished Lower Level

FM RM – Family Room

FML – Formal

FNCD YD – Fenced Yard

Foyr – Foyer

Fp, Fpl, Fplc – Fireplace

Fpgas – Gas Fireplace

FR – Family room

FSBO – For Sale by Owner

FXR – Fixer Upper

G/A – Garage, Attached

GAR – Garage

GARB – Garbage

GAROP – Garage Door Opener

GLF – Golf Course

GLFP – Gas Log Fireplace

GMT Kitchen – Gourmet Kitchen

GRNO – Ground Maintenance

G-RNG – Gas Range

HB – Half Bath (toilet + sink)

HBR – Harbor

HDWD – Hardwood

HIST – Historical District

HOA – Homeowner's Association

HP – Heat Pump

HPWA – Water/Air Heat Pump

HRS – Horses Allowed

HSF – Heated Square Feet

HTUB – Hot Tub

HUD Department of Housing and Urban Development

HVAC – Heating, Ventilation And Air Conditioning

HW – Hot Water

HWH – Hot Water Heater

IGSP – In-Ground Sprinkler

INGRD PL – In-Ground Pool

INLW – In-Law Suite
INT – Intercom
JTUB – Jetted Tub
LFT – Loft
LR – Living Room
LRG – Large
LTV – Loan-To-Value
MAR – Marble
MBA – Master Bedroom w/Bath
MBRFP – Master Bedroom w/FP
MCOA – Min $ on Assumption
MEIK – Modern Eat-In Kitchen
MIC – Mint Condition (like new or new)
MK – Modern Kitchen
MLS – Multiple Listing Service
MO – Month
MOPOA – Monthly POA Fee
MRSH – Marsh
MSN – Masonry
Mstr – Master Bedroom
MTG – Mortgage
MULTI – 3+ Car Garage
MWV – Microwave Oven
MYOB – Mind Your Own Business
NAR – National Association of Realtors
NAT GS HT – Natural Gas Heat
NBHD – Neighborhood
NGS – Natural Gas
NONQ – Non-Qualifying
NYSAR – New York State Association of Realtors
O/F – Owner Finance
OA – Owner Agent

OBO – Or Best Offer
OCN – Ocean
OFC – Office/Study
OFF – Off-Street Parking
OP – Occupancy Permit
OVER – Oversized Garage
OWN – Owner Financing
P&S – Purchase and sale
PAN – Pantry
PAR – Partially Fenced
PAT – Patio
PERM – Perm Attic Stairs
PGS – Propane
PICK – Picket Fence
PILE – Pilings
PITI – Principal, Interest, Taxes, and Insurance
PL – Swimming Pool
PL/A – Above-Ground Pool
PL/1 – In-Ground Pool
PLAY – Playground
PMI – Private Mortgage Insurance
PMP – Well Pump
POA – Power of Attorney
POR, POR-S – Porch/Screened
PROP HT – Propane Heat
PRQ – Parquet
PRTL – Partial
PRV, PVCY FENCE – Privacy Fence
PULL – Pull-Down Attic Stair
R/OPT – Rent w/Opt-Buy
RAD – Radiant Heat
RDR – Radiator

REC – Recreation Room
REF – Refrigerator
REL – Related to Seller
RELO – Relocation office
RNCH – Ranch
RTO – Rent to Own
RV PRKG – RV Parking
RVR – River
SAT – Satellite Dish
SCRND PORCH – Screened Porch
SD – Security Deposit
SEC – Security System
SEC SYS – Security System
SEW – Sewer
SHNG – Shingle
SHOP – Workshop
SKY – Skylights
SLT – Slate
SMB – Split Master Bedroom
SMP – Sump Pump
SN – Senior
SPC – Drive Parking Spaces
SPDED – Special Warranty Deed
SPKLR – Sprinkler
SPLT – Split-Level
SQ FT – Square Feet
SD/W – Storm Doors & Windows
SRO – Single Room Occupancy
STA – State
STOR – Assigned Storage
STR – On-Street Parking
SUN – Sun Room

SWR – Sewer

TEN – Tennis Court

TOWN – Town House

TRAD – Traditional

TRAN – Transitional

TRC – Trash Compactor

TRSH – Trash Pickup

TXS – Taxes

U/G SPRK – Underground Sprinkler

UNO – Unit Number

UTCL – Utility Closet

UTLVL – Utility Room Level

UTRM – Utility Room

VYL – Vinyl

W/D – Washer/Dryer

W/D HKUP – Washer/Dryer hookup

W/W CRPT – Wall-to-Wall Carpet

WAR – Warranty Plan

WBFP – Wood-Burning Fireplace

WBS – Wood-Burning Stove

WD PNL – Wood paneling

WDSTV – Wood-Burning Stove

WF – Waterfront

WHF – Whole House Fan

WHKP – Washer Hookup

WIN – Window/Wall Unit

WINDT – Window Treatment

WLKIN – Walk-in Closet

WSH – Washer

WTR – Water

WTR PD – Water paid

YD – Yard

REAL ESTATE AGENT CERTIFICATIONS & ABBREVIATIONS

ABR – Accredited Buyer Representative

AMO – Accredited Management Organization

CBR – Certified Buyer Representative

CHMS – Certified Home Marketing Specialist

CLHMS – Certified Luxury Home Marketing Specialist

CNS – Certified Negotiation Specialist

CPM – Certified Property Manager

CRB – Certified Real Estate Broker

CRS – Certified Residential Specialist

e-PRO – Internet Professional

GRES – Graduate Real Estate Society

GRI – Graduate REALTOR® Institute

NAR – National Association of Realtors

REALTOR® – Member of the National Association of Realtors

REBNY – Real Estate Board of New York

RPAC – Realtors Political Action Committee

SRES – Senior Real Estate Specialist

NEXT STEPS

We offer resources and support to help readers continue their journey towards financial freedom.

Free Downloads: Head over to www.reedgoossens.com/books to check out all the free downloads mentioned in this book.

Podcast: Go to iTunes, Soundcloud, Stitcher, or Google Play and subscribe to the *Investing in the US* podcast and continue learning from my incredible guests as they share their experiences.

Deal Analytica: Head over to www.dealanalytica.com or those readers who want real-time help underwriting their deals. This service is like having a full-time analyst working for you but for a fraction of the cost.

Facebook Page: Go to www.facebook.com/InvestingintheUS and join the community of other like-minded entrepreneurs for real-time inspiration.

YouTube: Check out all the recorded podcasts at www.youtube.com/c/ReedGoossens1 and continue learning from my incredible guests.

A QUICK FAVOR PLEASE?

Before you go can I ask you for a quick favor?

Good, I knew I could count on you.

Would you please leave this book a review on Amazon?

I promise it won't take long and will help this book reach more readers just like you.

Thank you for reading, thank you for your time, and thank you so much for being part of the journey.

–Reed

ABOUT THE AUTHOR

Top 10 things you didn't know about Reed:

1. I am Qualified chartered structural and civil engineer; worked on the 2012 Olympic Games in London, UK.

2. Spent a year in the south of France working as a deck-hand for the world's wealthiest businessmen on their super yachts.

3. Sailed across the Atlantic from Monaco to Antigua (Caribbean)—most incredible experience of my life!

4. I met my wife on the beaches in Spain whilst back packing around Europe in 2009.

5. Host of the Investing in the US podcast—the No. 1 podcast of investors looking to break into the US market.

6. I have travelled to over 30 countries, including trekking to Machu Picchu in Peru.

7. Hugely passionate amount rugby union. Favorite team: The Wallabies (when they win), Australia's national team.

8. Author of the book—*The 4P Rule: The Art & Science of Raising Capital Like a Pro.*

9. Been involved in the acquisition of over $150 mill worth of real estate since moving to the US back in 2012.

10. Personally controls over $100 mill of multifamily real estate.

CPSIA information can be obtained
at www.ICGtesting.com
Printed in the USA
BVHW030258311218
536761BV00001B/362/P